16 EXTRAORDINARY AMERICANS WITH DISABILITIES

NANCY LOBB

J. WESTON
WALCH
PUBLISHER
Portland, Maine

Photo Credits

Laura Bridgman	Dover Pictorial Archive
John Wesley Powell	Dover Pictorial Archive, Courtesy New-York Historical Society
Washington Roebling	Dover Pictorial Archive, Courtesy John A. Roebling's Sons Corporation
Franklin D. Roosevelt	Dover Pictorial Archive, Courtesy Library of Congress
Walt Disney	© Bettmann/CORBIS
Glenn Cunningham	© Bettmann/CORBIS
Roy Campanella	© 1997 by Photo File, Inc.
Bernard Bragg	Courtesy of Bernard Bragg
Ray Charles	AP/WIDE WORLD PHOTOS
Arthur Ashe	AP/WIDE WORLD PHOTOS
Cher	AP/WIDE WORLD PHOTOS
Ann Bancroft	AP/WIDE WORLD PHOTOS
Mark Wellman	AP/WIDE WORLD PHOTOS
Chris Burke	Courtesy of Marian Burke

1   2   3   4   5   6   7   8   9   10

ISBN 0-8251-4249-0

Copyright © 2001
J. Weston Walch, Publisher
P. O. Box 658 • Portland, Maine 04104-0658

Printed in the United States of America

Contents

Introduction

> The United States has come a long way in its understanding of disability. We know that disability is a natural part of life. We have begun to build a world that is accessible. No longer do we accept buildings that are not accessible, which is a "keep out" sign for the disabled.
>
> —Bob Dole, speech to the U.S. Senate, April 4, 1995

Millions of Americans have some type of disability. Some disabilities are easy to see. But other disabilities are invisible, like learning disabilities.

Many people with disabilities have overcome the odds against them. They have done great things. They have learned to concentrate on the things that they can do and work around the things that they cannot do. They have shown great courage as they moved forward with their lives.

The 16 Americans with disabilities whose stories are told in this book are outstanding examples. These Americans have made a difference in the story of the United States.

In this book you will read the stories of 16 Americans with disabilities who made extraordinary contributions to our nation. The stories include:

- Laura Bridgman, the first deaf-blind child to be educated

- John Wesley Powell, the one-armed schoolteacher who explored the Colorado River and the Grand Canyon

- Washington Roebling, the engineer who built the Brooklyn Bridge while very ill and in great pain from caisson disease

- Franklin D. Roosevelt, the 32nd president of the United States, who was unable to walk because of polio

- Katharine Hathaway, an artist and writer who made a life for herself in spite of being physically disabled.

- Walt Disney, a cartoonist and filmmaker who was called a "slow learner" as a child

- Glenn Cunningham, the greatest American miler of his time, who was badly burned as a boy

- Roy Campanella, one of the most famous catchers in baseball, who was paralyzed in a car accident

- Bernard Bragg, a deaf mime artist and actor

- Ray Charles, a blind singer who is known as the "genius of soul"

- Arthur Ashe, a tennis player who died of AIDS

- Cher, a successful singer and actress who is dyslexic

- Connie Briscoe, a best-selling author who lost her hearing at the age of 30

- Ann Bancroft, a woman with dyslexia who was the first woman to reach the North and the South Poles

- Mark Wellman, a paraplegic who has climbed mountains

- Chris Burke, an actor who has Down syndrome

The motto on the Great Seal of the United States reads *E Pluribus Unum.* That is Latin for "out of many, one." The United States is made up of people of different races, creeds, genders, ages, and disablilities. I hope you will enjoy reading about these 16 Americans with disabilities who have made a difference.

—Nancy Lobb

Laura Bridgman
Teacher

Everyone has heard the story of Helen Keller. But many do not know the story of Laura Bridgman. Laura was the first deaf-blind child to learn language. Laura's work paved the way for Helen Keller's success 50 years later.

Laura Bridgman was born on December 21, 1829. She was a pretty baby with bright blue eyes. Laura was a bright and happy child.

When she was one and one-half years old, Laura became ill with **scarlet fever.** For seven weeks she had a very high fever. She had to stay in bed in a dark room for five months. It was a year before she could walk again. Her two older sisters and older brother all died from the same illness.

Laura Bridgman

Slowly, Laura got stronger. She was out of danger. But things were still not right. It became clear that she could neither see nor hear. Her senses of smell and taste were nearly gone. Laura was in her own silent, dark world. No one could reach her. And she could not reach out to anyone else.

Laura played by herself. Sometimes she held an old boot that she treated like a doll. She followed her mother around. She copied what her mother did. In this way she learned to knit, mend, and clean. Still, it was hard for her parents to give her the time she needed. As farmers, they had many chores to do all day long. Plus, there were two younger children to care for.

Laura got the help she needed from a neighbor. Asa Tenney was an unusual man. He spent his days wandering in the woods and fields. He had no family or friends. He did not fit in anywhere. But when he met Laura, he knew he had found someone who needed him.

Asa Tenney spent every day with Laura. She went with him as he walked about outdoors. He taught her about the animals and plants that they found as they walked. He opened the world to her through her sense of touch.

The two made up their own sign language so that they could "talk" to each other. Soon Laura's hands were never still. She used them to replace her missing senses.

Laura was no longer lonely. She wanted to learn. Asa Tenney's time and love had done a great work. The strange old man had laid a firm base for Laura's later success.

By the time Laura was seven, she had become hard to control. She minded only her father. When he wanted her to stop doing something, he would stamp very hard on the floor. Laura could feel the floor **vibrate.** She knew she must stop at once.

One day, Mr. Bridgman hired a college student to help him. The young man soon met Laura. He was amazed to see that a child with so many problems did not just sit in a chair all day. Instead, she moved about the house and farm eager to learn and to find out what was going on.

Upon returning to college, the student told his teacher, Dr. Mussey, about Laura. Dr. Mussey went to see Laura. He gave her simple tests. Later he wrote a report about her. In it he listed the things Laura could do. He ended his report by wondering if the child could be **educated.**

Dr. Samuel Gridley Howe read Dr. Mussey's report. He was the director of the Perkins School for the Blind near Boston. He was thrilled to learn about Laura. He had always wanted to teach a deaf-blind child to understand language. This had never been done before. At the time these children were thought to be unable to learn. After all, how could they learn words if they couldn't hear or see?

Dr. Howe thought it could be done. He had worked on some ideas for how to do it. Laura sounded like a good child to work with. She was bright. And she wanted to learn.

On October 12, 1837, Laura went to live at the Perkins School. She was eight years old. It was not an easy change for her. She did not understand why she had to leave her home. She did not understand why her mother and father were not staying there with her. There was no way anyone could tell her what was going on. But people were kind to her. After a few weeks, Laura was happy in her new home.

Dr. Howe began Laura's lessons. On a table he put a key, a spoon, a knife, a fork, a book, and a cup. Dr. Howe handed Laura the key. She felt it and knew what it was.

On the key, Dr. Howe had placed a label. The letters K, E, and Y were written on it in raised letters. Dr. Howe guided Laura's fingers over the letters. Of course, she had no idea what they were. He repeated this process with the other things on the table.

The letters Dr. Howe used were not the **braille** letters we know today. Braille had just been invented in 1829 in France. It was not in wide use at this time outside of France. Instead, Dr. Howe used a raised alphabet, which was easy to feel.

Soon Laura was able to pick out a label and put it on the right object. She was playing a matching game. This was progress. But Laura did not yet understand that the letters spelled the name of the object.

Even so, Dr. Howe was pleased. He felt sure now that he would be able to teach Laura. The only question in his mind was how long it would take.

He wrote, "Laura was like a person alone and helpless in a deep, dark, still pit. I was letting down a cord and [moving] it about in hopes she might find it. [I hoped she would then grab] it and be drawn up by it into the light of day and human [company]."

The lessons went on twice a day. Laura loved them and never wanted to stop. One day Dr. Howe tried something new. He cut the labels into separate letters. Laura quickly learned to put the letters in order to spell the words. Soon Laura could spell the names of all the objects she had learned.

Next, Laura learned to finger spell. Of course, she could not see the shapes of the letters. The letters had to be formed in her hand. That way she could feel them. Laura learned to finger spell the names of the objects she had learned.

Laura was still just learning by memory. She had no understanding of what she was doing. She just learned what to do on command. There was no meaning in the letters.

Suddenly one day everything made sense to her. She realized that Dr. Howe had been showing her that things had names. She understood what all the "strange" things she had been learning meant. Everything had a name. These names could be spelled with letters or finger spelling.

Howe later wrote, "I could fix upon the moment when this truth dawned upon her mind. At once her face lighted up with a human expression." Laura was no longer learning without understanding. She had found a way to link herself to other human beings. Laura had grabbed the rope and was coming out into the daylight.

Now Laura began to learn quickly. She asked for the name of every object she felt. She kept her teacher busy all day long telling her the names of everything. Dr. Howe had to ask her to be quiet so her teacher could eat dinner. In a few days she had learned the names of over 100 things. Names of things (nouns) were the easiest words for Laura to learn.

Next her teacher began to teach her action words, or verbs. First she learned the meaning of "open" and "shut." Next she learned other verbs like "run," "walk," "sleep," "eat," and so on. Verbs were easy to learn if they could be acted out.

Other verbs were harder. It was a struggle to teach her words like "think" and "was." Dr. Howe and the other teachers sometimes got discouraged. But Laura never did. She thought it was all a great puzzle to be solved.

Adjectives came next. (An adjective is a word that describes nouns.) Laura learned words like "smooth," "sharp," "soft," and "hard." She went on to learn the other parts of speech too.

It was hard for Laura to learn the names of things she could not touch. Putting words together in the right order to make sentences was hard too. Since she could not hear others talking, she had to learn how to put a sentence together by learning rules. It was not easy!

Over the years, Laura learned other subjects. She learned math and geography. She learned history. She studied reading and writing.

She learned to write on paper with **grooves** on it. The grooves helped her keep her letters straight. Laura enjoyed writing letters to her parents. She also wrote to friends who had visited her at the school.

One thing Laura never learned was how to speak. Instead, she talked to others using sign language.

Dr. Howe kept careful notes on his work with Laura. Each year he **published** a report about her progress. He made his writing very interesting to read. People all over the world looked forward to reading his next report.

Dr. Howe held a monthly open house at the school. Anyone could come and see how the blind were educated. He invited state **legislators** to come see the work he was doing. He hoped they would send more tax money to support the school.

By 1839, thousands of people were coming to the open houses. Most of them came to see Laura Bridgman. Crowds gathered to watch Laura do math, sew, or write with paper and pencil.

In 1842, when Laura was 13, Charles Dickens came all the way from England to see her. He was a famous writer who had read about Laura. (Some of his books are *Oliver Twist, David Copperfield,* and *A Christmas Carol.*) After visiting her at the school, he wrote about her in his book *American Notes.* Since Dickens was widely read, Laura's fame quickly spread.

Forty years later, a woman in Alabama read *American Notes.* She was the mother of another deaf-blind child, Helen Keller. When

Mrs. Keller read of Dr. Howe's work with Laura, she wrote to the Perkins Institute for help. They sent a teacher: Anne Sullivan.

Anne Sullivan spent long hours studying the notes about how Laura had been taught. When she left for the Kellers, she took a doll for Helen. Laura Bridgman had made the clothes for the doll. Two years later, Helen and Anne Sullivan went to Perkins to meet Laura Bridgman.

Laura Bridgman lived at Perkins for 52 years. She earned some money through her sewing and knitting. People wanted to buy things made by the famous Laura Bridgman.

Laura also helped teach other deaf-blind children who came to the school. She taught the blind children how to sew. She got letters from all over the world from people who had read her story.

Laura Bridgman died at Perkins on May 24, 1889. She was 59 years old.

At Perkins, a candle had been lit in Laura's dark world. This light was passed along to other deaf-blind children around the world. No longer would they live their lives in silent darkness. Laura Bridgman had led the way out.

Remembering the Facts

1. How did Laura lose her sight and hearing?

2. Why was it hard for her parents to give her enough attention?

3. How did Asa Tenney help Laura?

4. What problem did the Bridgmans have when Laura was seven years old?

5. Why did Dr. Howe want to work with Laura?

6. What were some of the first words Laura learned?

7. How did Laura learn to finger spell?

8. Name something that was hard for Laura to learn.

9. What famous writer wrote about Laura?

10. How did Laura's story help Helen Keller?

Understanding the Story

11. Why do you think it would be hard for a child who was deaf and blind from a young age to learn?

12. Why do you think Laura was so hard to control as a young child?

Getting the Main Idea

Why do you think Laura Bridgman is a good role model for young people?

Applying What You've Learned

Choose a word for something you cannot touch. Tell how you might teach this word to a deaf-blind person. Some examples are: happy, sad, on, in, right, alone . . .

John Wesley Powell
Explorer

The American Indians feared it. They said it had waterfalls hundreds of feet high. Huge whirlpools swallowed anything coming down it. Waterspouts were said to fly up from it and knock birds out of the air. In places it was said that it disappeared underground. Its roar was said to deafen people.

What was this fearful thing? It was the Colorado River!

John Wesley Powell had heard all these stories and more. He wanted to learn the truth about the river. In 1869, the river's 1,000-mile course was mostly unknown.

John Wesley Powell

But John Wesley Powell had decided to travel the length of the Colorado River. He planned to chart its course. He would study the plants, animals, and rocks he saw. He would keep a journal of all his findings.

On May 24, 1869, Powell and a group of nine men set out in four small boats. The whole country thought they were crazy. They thought they would never make it out alive.

After all, Powell was just a teacher. Not only that, he had only one arm. Powell didn't let that stop him. He took his little boats straight into the Grand Canyon of the Colorado. Three months later, he came through to tell his story. John Wesley Powell became an American hero.

John Wesley Powell was born on March 24, 1834, in Mount Morris, New York. When he was four years old, his family moved to Jackson, Ohio. His father was a preacher. He often spoke out against slavery. This made many people angry. Powell's classmates called him names. He was beaten. It became unsafe for him to go to school.

Powell's father sent him to live with George Crookham. Crookham was a farmer. But he was also a scientist and teacher. Crookham had a classroom in his home. But he loved teaching his students outside. There he talked to them about plants, animals, and landforms. Powell learned to see the whole world as a classroom.

Powell's father wanted him to become a preacher. But young Powell refused. He wanted to study science. So his father refused to pay for his **education.** This did not stop Powell. He left home. At the age of 12, he got a job on a large farm. When he got time, he read anything he could get his hands on. He saved his money. When he could, he took science courses.

When Powell was 18, he tried to get a teaching job. At first he was turned down. He was young and had no degree. But it was clear that he was well educated. He had taught himself and knew many subjects well. Powell landed his first teaching job.

School in those days followed the farm calendar. In the fall and winter, children went to school. In the spring and summer they worked on the farms. During that time, Powell ran rivers. He floated down the Mississippi all the way to New Orleans. He ran the Ohio River. He tried the Missouri. After that came the Illinois. Some summers he just hiked all summer. It was a great way to live!

This pattern ended when the Civil War began. In April 1861, Powell joined the Union army as a private. By fall, he had become a captain. At that time, he was given a leave to marry Emma Dean.

On April 6, 1862, Powell fought at the Battle of Shiloh. There he was shot in his right arm. The arm could not be saved. It had to be **amputated** at the elbow. Powell got better. He fought in nine other battles. But the stump of the arm gave him much pain. Before the war ended, Powell had earned the rank of major.

Finally, the war was over. Powell was hired as a professor of geology at Wesleyan University. Later he taught at Illinois State Normal University. He worked hard to improve their science courses. He also won a grant from the state legislature. With it, he set up the Illinois Natural Historical Society Museum at the college.

For two summers, Powell led groups of students on trips into the Colorado Rockies. On these trips, he heard wild stories about the Colorado River. He decided he would make a trip to explore the area.

He arranged for four small, strong boats to be made. Each was about 20 feet long. The boats had watertight places for food and supplies. Powell hired nine men willing to brave the unknown. They all met in the town of Green River, Wyoming.

On May 24, 1869, the group set out! The four boats, loaded heavily, started down the Green River. Powell stood in the lead boat. With his one arm, he waved to the people on shore. The last major **exploration** of the continental United States was under way.

For the first five days, the river ran quietly. The men used this time to learn to handle the boats. On May 27 they reached a spot where the Green River seemed to disappear into the mountains. The boats moved into the **gorge.** It was narrow with red and orange walls 1,200 feet high. The men named it Flaming Gorge.

Flaming Gorge was beautiful. But it was hard going. The water thundered. Huge rocks flashed past. The water towered high above them. The men tried to keep the boats pointed straight ahead.

Suddenly, the **rapids** ended. They were in quiet water. It was time to camp for the night. They had made it through their first **whitewater.** The men were excited but glad to be through it.

But Major Powell did not rest when they stopped. He climbed the **canyon** walls looking for **fossils.** Having one arm did not slow him down. He went straight up the steep walls. He took measurements with scientific instruments. He used a **sextant** to find their location. He used a **barometer** to check their **altitude.** He recorded the direction of the river. He noted the distance traveled each day. All this information would be needed to map the area.

Since they were in unmapped lands, they named the places they passed. Powell noted all this in his journal. Most of the names are still in use today.

Things were going well. The river was rough enough to be exciting but not too dangerous. There were good places to camp at night. And there was plenty of wild game to shoot as they went.

This changed when they reached the place they named Lodore Canyon. Here they had their first disaster. On a bad stretch of river, one of the boats crashed into a rock. The men were saved. But the boat was lost. Now everyone had to crowd into three boats. Also, one fourth of the food and supplies had been lost.

The men went on. But the boats were beginning to leak. Bumping against the rocks had opened small cracks in the wood. Everything got wet, even the food. The flour was damp. The bacon got moldy. There was less and less fresh game. Soon everyone was hungry. To make matters worse, there were no good campsites. Strong winds blew down the rocky canyons, making it hard to sleep. By day, the sun burned their skin. But they kept on.

Finally, on June 28, they came to the mouth of the Uinta River. Forty miles up the river was an American Indian **agency.** Powell and some men hiked to the agency. They were able to get some fresh supplies. They also mailed letters. Everyone who got the letters was surprised. Newspaper stories had been telling of the group's deaths for weeks!

At the agency, one member of the group left. He had had enough adventure. The rest of the group went on its way.

One day, Powell was climbing to the canyon rim 2,000 feet above the river. He did this often. He wanted to collect fossils and rocks and take scientific measurements. The men were always amazed by how the one-armed major climbed the steep cliffs.

But this time Powell got in trouble. High up the cliff, he jumped onto a narrow ledge. Then he found that he could go no farther. He held onto the cliff with his one hand. But he could not turn around to jump back. He was stuck.

Luckily, this time another man had gone with Powell. The man climbed above Powell. But he could not reach down to the Major. Finally, he hit on the idea of taking off his long underwear. He held this down to Powell. Powell climbed up the "rope" and was saved.

On July 17, they came to the spot where the Green River joins the Colorado River. Now the river was much larger. The rapids were even bigger. Solid waves of white water rose 15 feet above the boats. Oars were smashed on the rocks. In Cataract Canyon, one boat flipped. The men clung to the boat until it reached calm water. In Marble Canyon the boats were beaten so badly that they had to stop for repairs. Again and again the major with one arm climbed the canyon walls to get pitch to mend the boats.

They reached the entrance of the Grand Canyon on August 13. The canyon became deeper and narrower. It was 5,000 feet (nearly a mile) deep. For most of the day the steep walls shut out the sun. In many places the river filled the canyon from one side to the other. Often, there was no place to land the boats.

On August 27, they came to the worst rapids they had ever seen. There was no riverbank at all. There was no way out. They would either have to climb out of the canyon and go home or run the fearful rapids.

Powell did not want to give up. They had come so far and risked so much. But three of the men did not want to risk what lay ahead. They decided to hike out. The others stayed with Powell. Now there were six men left. The next morning they loaded the two best boats and started off.

At once the river carried them off. The water moved faster and faster. The rapids battered them. One of the men was nearly killed. By far, these were the worst rapids they had seen. But on August 29, the canyon widened. Without warning the steep cliffs were behind them. They began to drift along on a gentle current.

The next day, they were surprised when a fisherman called to them from the bank. He had been asked to stand at that spot. He was supposed to watch for bodies or pieces of wrecked boats floating downstream. After all, the world wanted to know the fate of Powell and his men. Quickly the fisherman took charge of the tired group. Soon Powell and his men were fed and rested.

But the three men who had hiked out of the canyon had not been so lucky. They had made camp near the rim of the Grand Canyon. While sleeping, they had been killed by a band of American Indians. They were mistaken for three men who had killed an American Indian woman nearby.

The great trip had ended! But John Wesley Powell was not done exploring. He went to Congress. He wanted to get money to explore more of the land around the Colorado River. During the years 1871–1879, Powell explored the canyons of Colorado, Arizona, Utah, and New Mexico. He named rivers, valleys, and canyons. Powell was named head of the U.S. Geographical and Geological Survey in 1881.

Powell reported on the plants and animals of the area. He studied the soil and the water supply. He collected fossils. He collected photos of the American Indians. He recorded information about their languages and customs. He wrote down their legends and history. He saved boxes of things the American Indians made. Weapons. Pottery. Clothing. All were sent to the Smithsonian Institution in Washington, D.C.

In the spring of 1878, Powell published a book called *Report on the Lands of the Arid Region of the United States.* (**Arid** means "dry.") In this book, Powell talked about changes that were needed to government laws about the West. He had a plan for how the dry lands in the West should be managed. Some areas were too dry to farm but would be good for cattle.

Powell had become the best-known scientist in the United States. He was the only person who questioned the way the West was being developed. He knew it was important to use the water in the dry West carefully. But the government did not listen to most of his ideas. Powell resigned as head of the survey in 1894. It was not until after his death that people saw that his ideas had been right. His plan then became the basis for all future land reform laws.

On September 23, 1902, John Wesley Powell died. He was 68 years old. In 1969, on the 100th anniversary of his running of the Colorado River, a stamp was issued. It showed Powell standing in his boat, leading the way into the rapids. He was waving with his one good arm!

Remembering the Facts

1. Describe one story that was told about the Colorado River.

2. What disability did Powell have?

3. Why did Powell have to stop attending school as a boy?

4. How did Powell get most of his education?

5. What disaster happened in Lodore Canyon?

6. What scientific measurements did Powell take on the trip?

7. What happened to the three men who left Powell at the Grand Canyon?

8. What government agency did Powell later head?

9. What was the name of Powell's book?

10. What kind of information did Powell collect on the American Indians?

Understanding the Story

11. How do you think George Crookham set Powell on the road he followed through life?

12. Powell became famous because of his explorations. How do you think he showed the same courage in his later years?

Getting the Main Idea

Why do you think John Wesley Powell is a good role model for young people?

Applying What You've Learned

Why do you think the Colorado River area was the last unexplored area of the continental United States?

Washington Roebling
Engineer

It was May 24, 1883. Thousands of people filled the streets of New York City and Brooklyn. Everyone was excited. It was the opening day for the new Brooklyn Bridge!

At last it was done! It was the longest **suspension** bridge in the world. It was over a mile long: 5,862 feet in all. Its two towers were taller than any other buildings in sight. It had taken 14 years of hard, dangerous work to finish the bridge. And it had cost $18 million. People were calling it the eighth wonder of the world!

Washington Roebling

President Chester Arthur arrived at 2:00 P.M. He got out of his carriage and walked across the bridge. Everyone cheered. Cannons were fired from Navy ships on the river. Factories and boats blew their whistles. Church bells rang.

A total of 150,300 people crossed the bridge that day. Each person paid one penny to cross. Cars crossing the bridge had to pay a nickel.

But one man couldn't join the fun. In a house close by, overlooking the bridge, Washington Roebling sat watching from his bedroom window. He was the chief **engineer** of the bridge. But Roebling was completely **disabled.** He had **caisson disease** from working long hours on the base of the bridge far beneath the river. For 11 of the 14 years it had taken to build the bridge, he had not been able to leave his room. Yet he was able to finish the bridge.

Washington Roebling was born on May 26, 1837, in Saxonburg, Pennsylvania. His father, John Roebling, was a stern man. He was often away from home. He was an engineer who built bridges (a civil engineer). He had little time for his family.

When Washington was seven years old, he was sent to boarding school in Pittsburgh. It was a 25-mile trip by wagon. This was a long, hard trip on the poor roads of that day. So Washington did not get home often.

John Roebling moved his family to Trenton, New Jersey when Washington was 12. He built a factory that made wire cable. He also built bridges using this cable.

John Roebling became world famous when he built the Niagara Falls Railway suspension bridge. This bridge **spanned** 821 feet below the falls. From then on, he had more work than he could handle.

Washington Roebling wanted to build bridges, too. He went to Rensselaer Polytechnic Institute to study **engineering.** It was not an easy school. Sixty-five students began their studies at the same time as Washington. Only 12 **graduated.**

Washington Roebling went to work with his father. They were building a suspension bridge in Pittsburgh. It took two years to complete this bridge. During this time, John Roebling often left to work on other projects. While he was gone, Washington would be in charge of the job.

In April 1861, the Civil War began. One night at dinner, John Roebling looked across the table at Washington. He asked, "Don't you think you've stretched your legs under my (table) long enough?" Without a word, Washington got up and left the house. He joined the Union army.

The army needed Washington Roebling to build bridges. He had to work fast. Often he worked under enemy fire. Some of the bridges were destroyed soon after they were built. But the fearless young man quickly rebuilt them.

Washington's fame grew. He built a 1,200-foot suspension bridge across the Rappahannock River. He built another across the Shenandoah River at Harper's Ferry.

Another of Washington's duties during the war was going up in a hot air balloon every morning. From the air he was to watch the enemy and learn what they were up to. Washington Roebling won three awards for bravery. He ended the war with the rank of colonel.

In 1865, Washington Roebling married Emily Warren. Emily was a strong woman. She would need that strength to deal with the problems that lay ahead of her.

About this time, John Roebling was planning a bridge to join New York City and Brooklyn. A bridge to join the two cities had been needed for years. Many plans had been drawn up. But none of them would work.

The main problem was the East River. It was not really a river at all. It was a narrow channel where the tide swept in and out. The waters ran deep and fast. It would not be easy to build a bridge there.

But a bridge was badly needed! Many people living in Brooklyn worked in New York. The only way to get there was by **ferry.** Ferries crossed the river every day. They were crowded and dirty. Often there was a long wait to get on. Storms, fog, or ice on the river meant the ferry did not run at all. The delays could last for days.

In 1867, John Roebling was hired by the state of New York to build the bridge. He drew up plans. The bridge would have both a road and a railroad. It would also have a walkway for people to stroll on and enjoy the view.

John Roebling sent Washington to Europe in 1868. Washington talked with leading engineers in England, France, and Germany. There he was to study new ways of building **foundations** for bridges. Washington decided on an experimental method. It was called the "caisson method."

On June 28, 1869, John Roebling was looking over the bridge site. He was standing on the dock near the water. A ferry bumped into the dock. His foot was crushed. His toes had to be **amputated.** Soon **tetanus** set in. He died on July 22, 1869.

This sad event left Washington Roebling, 32, in charge of building the largest bridge in the world. He left the growing wire rope business in Trenton for others to run. He had to spend all his time on the Brooklyn Bridge.

The Brooklyn Bridge was to be a suspension bridge. A suspension bridge is a bridge in which the roadway is hung from cables. The cables are anchored at both ends and supported by towers.

The Brooklyn Bridge would have two towers. One would be on each side of the river. Each tower would be 276 feet tall. Sixteen-inch thick cables would be hung from the towers. These would hold up the roadway. The huge cables would be long enough to reach all the way across the river.

Work would begin with the Brooklyn tower. To support the huge bridge, they first had to dig down to solid rock. On the rock the foundations of the towers would be laid.

Building the foundation far below the water's surface called for a special method. At a shipyard a huge caisson was built. It looked like an upside-down box without a lid. It was 168 feet long and 102 feet wide. Inside it was nine and one-half feet deep. The walls were very thick. They were covered with tin. The caisson had to be watertight.

The caisson was towed down the river. It was sunk at the spot where the tower was to be built. Pumps pushed the water out of the caisson. Now it was like an empty box full of air.

There were two air lock shafts in the roof of the caisson. Through these, men entered the caisson. This is where they would work every day. Inside, they used picks to break up rocks. They shoveled dirt. The rocks and dirt were hauled up the air lock and carried off.

For this heavy work, the men were paid $2.25 a day. This was a very high wage at the time. But most men could not stand the job for long.

The workers, called sandhogs, dug deeper into the riverbed. The caisson sank as they dug. They went down about 6–18 inches a week. When it had sunk 45 feet below the surface, the caisson struck solid rock. Then the caisson was filled with cement. The tower was then built on top of it.

In September 1871, work began on the New York tower. This time the bedrock was even deeper under the river. This led to a big problem. Many workers started getting sick. A few died. No one could figure out why.

The workers felt all right while they were inside the caisson. It was when they went back to the surface that they became ill. Some became faint. Others felt numb. Often they had blurred vision. Some men got bad cramps in their legs and stomachs. They began calling the illness "caisson disease."

The doctors did not know what was wrong with the men. Today we know the cause of caisson disease, also called the bends. A person who breathes air under high pressure takes in extra **oxygen** and **nitrogen** from the air. The oxygen is not a problem. It is used by the body and does not build up in the blood. But nitrogen and other gases build up in the blood. The only way they can leave the body is out through the lungs. This process takes time. That is why divers today take safety stops on their way up to the surface.

When a person goes too quickly from a high-pressure area (such as far under water) to a low-pressure area (such as the surface), the nitrogen in the blood forms bubbles. The extra gas stays in the body after each time under pressure.

The most common symptom of the bends is pain. It is usually in the arm or leg joints. There may be weakness in an arm or leg. This may lead to **paralysis.** The ears may be affected. The person may be dizzy or have a loss of hearing. The person may feel very tired all the time.

In the first six months of 1872, 110 men were treated for the bends. Three of them died. Washington Roebling knew it was dangerous to work in the caisson. But the bridge had to be built! Washington Roebling spent more time in the caisson than any of the workers. He did not want to ask anyone to do something he was not willing to do.

He was a strong example for his men. But one day after 12 hours inside the caisson, he **collapsed.** He had to be carried out of the caisson in great pain. He nearly died. He finally improved a little. But his legs were **paralyzed.** He was in pain for the rest of his life. Roebling lost much of his sight and hearing. It was even hard for him to speak. Roebling was not able to go out to the bridge again.

Roebling remained alert. He directed the building from his bedroom. He used a **telescope** to watch the bridge's progress. He taught his wife Emily some engineering terms. She needed to understand some of the building process. That way she could carry Roebling's instructions to the foreman of the building crew.

All went on according to plan. Roebling directed the whole process without seeing it himself. He knew what was going on at all times and what had to be done next. He did this for 11 years until the bridge was completed.

Finally both towers were done. Next the four huge cables had to be hung. For the first time ever, steel wires were used. Steel had never been used to build a bridge or building. But Roebling knew that steel would be strong. It took years to make and hang the huge cables. The roadway was built and supported by the cables. The railroad tracks were laid. Finally, in 1883, the bridge was done.

After the bridge was done, Washington Roebling retired. In a few years he again took over as president of the wire rope company. He was still in great pain and poor health. But he kept his mind active.

Washington Roebling died on July 21, 1926, in Trenton, New Jersey. He was 89.

It has been over 100 years since the bridge was built. Today it is the second busiest bridge in New York City. Every day 144,000 cars and trucks cross it.

But it is more than just a bridge. It is more than just a beautiful sight. It is a symbol of engineering **genius.** It is also a symbol of one man's courage to follow his dream. No engineering job has ever been carried out under such difficult conditions.

Remembering the Facts

1. What two cities does the Brooklyn Bridge join?

2. Who was president of the United States when the bridge was completed?

3. Where did Washington Roebling get his engineering degree?

4. What work did he do for the army during the Civil War?

5. Why did the Brooklyn Bridge need to be built?

6. Who drew up the plans for the Brooklyn Bridge?

7. What work was done inside the caissons?

8. Why did many workers in the caissons get the bends?

9. How did Roebling direct the building after he became ill?

10. What metal was used to build the cables for the Brooklyn Bridge?

Understanding the Story

11. In 1964, the Brooklyn Bridge was named a National Historic Landmark. Why do you think it got this honor?

12. How do you think Emily Roebling showed great courage?

Getting the Main Idea

Why do you think Washington Roebling is a role model for young people today?

Applying What You've Learned

If the Brooklyn Bridge were being built today, how do you think the work might be easier than it was 100 years ago?

Franklin D. Roosevelt
President of the United States

Franklin D. Roosevelt was president from 1933–1945. He was elected four times, more than any other president. He led the country through some of its darkest days. The **Great Depression** and World War II took place during his years in the White House. And Roosevelt was the first elected leader of the United States with a disability.

Franklin Roosevelt was born at his family home in Hyde Park, New York on January 30, 1882. His parents owned a large home on 1,000 acres of land. Gardens and fields of grain covered the rolling hills. There were stables full of horses to ride.

Franklin D. Roosevelt

Franklin's brother Rosy was 26 years old when Franklin was born. So Franklin grew up as an only child. His loving parents gave him everything money could buy.

Franklin was a happy child. He loved riding and swimming. He learned to sail. He spent hours outdoors, learning the name of every tree, rock, and bird on the farm. He and his parents took many trips to Europe. Franklin did not often play with other children. But he got lots of attention from adults.

Franklin was home-schooled. His favorite subjects were history and geography. He learned to speak French and German. He learned carpentry. His hobbies were taking pictures and stamp collecting.

All of his life, Franklin liked to read. His favorite books were about the U.S. Navy. One day, his mother found him reading the dictionary. She asked what he was doing. He answered, "There are lots of words I don't understand." Then he added, "I am almost halfway through."

In 1896, Franklin left his sheltered world to attend Groton School. This was a **prep school** in Massachusetts. Only boys from rich families went to Groton.

At Groton, Franklin was a B and C student. He liked sports, but he wasn't much of an **athlete.** He did manage the school's baseball team one year. Roosevelt was not popular, but he did make some friends.

Franklin Roosevelt entered Harvard University in 1900. He studied history, government, English, and public speaking. But he didn't study very hard. His grades were mostly Cs. His fourth year he was editor of *The Harvard Crimson,* the school newspaper.

During Roosevelt's first year at Harvard, his father died. His mother moved into an apartment near Harvard to be near her son. Some students teased Roosevelt about being a "mama's boy."

Roosevelt was good to his mother. But he had his own ideas, some of which his mother did not like. One of these was his desire to run for office. The second was his romance with Eleanor Roosevelt, his fifth cousin. Roosevelt's mother did not like Eleanor.

Eleanor had an unhappy childhood. Her father drank too much. Her mother was unkind to her. Both of her parents had died by the time Eleanor was 10. Her grandmother raised her. Eleanor became a quiet, shy young woman.

Eleanor and Franklin were married in 1905. Franklin Roosevelt went on to Columbia Law School. He passed the bar exam. Then he began working on Wall Street. In the next 12 years, Eleanor had six children.

In 1910, Franklin Roosevelt ran for New York state **senator.** His cousin Teddy Roosevelt was a **Republican** and president of the United States. But Franklin ran as a **Democrat.** No one thought he had a chance to win. But he worked hard. He drove all over, making as many as 10 speeches a day. People liked his warm, friendly ways. He won easily, surprising everyone!

In 1912, Woodrow Wilson, a Democrat, became president. He asked Roosevelt to serve as his **assistant** secretary of the Navy. Franklin Roosevelt held this job for seven years. He learned much that would help him later as president. He inspected ships. He went down in subs. He worked hard to get new equipment for the Navy. He said, "I get my fingers into everything. There's no law against it."

In April 1917, the United States entered World War I. Roosevelt's job with the Navy became even more important. He had many decisions to make. He learned about how the Navy worked during a war. He toured the war zones and learned much firsthand knowledge.

In 1920, Roosevelt was **nominated** for vice president. He was running with James Cox. He dashed around the country making speeches. Roosevelt and Cox lost the election. But Roosevelt was not upset. He said, "The moment of defeat is the best time to lay plans for future victories."

In August 1921, Roosevelt was on vacation at his summer home. The Roosevelts and their six young children were having a great time. But one day, Roosevelt began to feel ill. He thought he had the flu. But it was much worse than that. He had **polio.** The disease left his legs **paralyzed.** He would never walk again.

But Roosevelt did not let polio defeat him. He promised himself he would not be helpless or sad. He designed a light wheel-chair from a kitchen chair. Using his strong arms, he learned to lift himself into any chair. He had a small car rebuilt so he could drive it without foot pedals.

Roosevelt had to wear thick steel braces. These weighed seven pounds each. They kept his legs straight so he could stand. Roosevelt learned to stand up, leaning against a table. Through all this, he never complained. He always kept a smile on his face. He never talked about his disability, even with his family. To him it was just a fact of life.

Polio was the greatest challenge of Roosevelt's life. All other problems would seem smaller after that. He once said, "If you had spent two years in bed trying to wiggle your big toe, after that anything else would seem easy!"

In 1924, Roosevelt heard about Warm Springs, Georgia. It was a health spa that had warm mineral water for swimming. The warm, heavy water kept him afloat. It eased his pain too. It helped so much that Roosevelt bought the spa. Over the next 20 years, he made it into a first-class center where other people with polio could be helped.

Later in 1924, Roosevelt was to give a speech at the Democratic National **Convention.** In it he was to nominate Al Smith for president. Roosevelt did not want to be seen in his wheelchair. So he "walked" to the stage. His son held one arm. He used a crutch in the other. Very, very slowly he struggled to the stage. The crowd held its breath. They were afraid he would fall. When he got to the front, he threw away his crutch. He held himself up by leaning on the stand. He gave his speech. When it was over, the crowd clapped for an hour and 13 minutes. It had been a rare act of courage.

It had also been part of Roosevelt's plan to hide the fact that he couldn't walk. He believed that if people thought he was a "cripple" he would never be elected to office. Many people helped him hide his disability. No reporter wrote that FDR could not walk. No photos were taken of him in his wheelchair.

In 1928, Roosevelt ran for governor of New York. He gave speeches all across New York. He won! He was elected again in 1930. He did a great job. As Al Smith said, "We do not elect him to do a handspring. The work of the governor is brain work."

In the 1920s America was the richest country in the world. Wages were the highest ever. People were getting rich in the stock market.

In October 1929, the stock market crashed. In a short time, 13 million people were out of work. People were going hungry. Long lines of people waited to be fed at soup kitchens. Many lost their homes. Millions wandered around the country looking for work.

Banks closed. People lost everything they had. The Great Depression had begun.

It was during this hard time that Franklin Roosevelt first ran for president. In his speeches, he talked about only one thing. He told people his plan to save the country. Then he would say, "I pledge you, I pledge myself, to a new deal for the American people." After this, the band would play the song "Happy Days are Here Again." Roosevelt won by a landslide.

In 1933, Roosevelt took office. He gave his **inaugural** address. It gave hope to the country. He made it clear he was a strong leader. He was calm and confident that things would get better.

Roosevelt got right to work. The very next day he had a plan to save the country's banks. During the next 104 days, FDR pushed bill after bill through Congress. This time became known as The Hundred Days. It also marked the beginning of the "New Deal."

FDR started many programs. "Do something," he said. "If it works, do it some more. And if it does not work, then do something else."

Roosevelt had the support of the people. Just one week after taking office, he gave his first Fireside Chat on radio. With millions of Americans listening, he explained his plans. He asked for everyone's help. He was so warm and friendly, everyone felt he was talking to them. During his 12 years in the White House, FDR gave 30 of these talks.

One of his ideas was the WPA (**Works Progress Administration**). The WPA hired many people: teachers, artists, writers, and builders, to name a few. It paid them to work on 250,000 projects. These included building hospitals, recording music, doing paintings, and so on. By 1941, the WPA had put eight million people back to work.

One of FDR's favorite programs was the CCC (**Civilian Conservation Corps**). The CCC hired men between the ages of 18 and 25. They planted trees. They fought fires. They improved America's parks. They built dams. And they got back their faith in America.

FDR was very popular. In 1936, he was reelected by a landslide. Roosevelt had become the hero of the working class. He pledged to work for "the young people, the crippled, the blind, the mothers, those who are out of work, and the elderly. . . . For these, we have only just begun to fight."

In 1939, World War II began in Europe. Most Americans wanted to stay out of the war. Roosevelt had planned to retire from office. But now he felt he must run again. He was elected to a third term in 1940.

In 1941, the Japanese bombed Pearl Harbor, Hawaii. The United States was forced to enter World War II. Now, Roosevelt had to spend most of his time on winning the war.

In 1944, the war was still raging. Roosevelt was tired. But the people still wanted him as president. "All that is within me cries to go back to my home on the Hudson River," said FDR. But he said he would serve again "like a good soldier."

Roosevelt was elected to a fourth term. He was to serve only three months of that term. In fact, Roosevelt did not live to see the war end. On April 12, 1945, he was resting at Warm Springs when he had a stroke and died. He was 63 years old.

Roosevelt had held the nation together during its darkest days. Indeed, he was a symbol of hope. Few other presidents equaled his impact. Under his leadership, the United States became the world leader it is today.

Few people know that Roosevelt also founded the March of Dimes. This group raised millions of dollars to find a cure for polio. On April 12, 1955, the March of Dimes announced the first polio **vaccine.** Dr. Jonas Salk had made the vaccine. Today, polio has been wiped out in the United States.

In January 2001, a statue of FDR in his wheelchair was unveiled at the FDR Memorial. Many disabled Americans were there. They wheeled their chairs next to that of FDR to pose for pictures. One person in the crowd said, "I took courage from him. I believe that since he was able to do what he did, the sky's the limit for me."

Remembering the Facts

1. Describe Roosevelt's home in Hyde Park, New York.

2. What subject did Roosevelt most like to read about?

3. To which party did Roosevelt belong?

4. What was the first office Roosevelt ran for?

5. How did his job as assistant secretary of the Navy help Roosevelt when he became president?

6. What disease did Roosevelt get in 1921?

7. What was happening in the United States when Roosevelt first ran for president?

8. What were the Fireside Chats?

9. Why did Roosevelt run for a third term as president?

10. How many times was Roosevelt elected president?

Understanding the Story

11. No pictures were taken of Roosevelt in his wheelchair. Why do you think that was so?

12. Roosevelt tried to hide his disability. Do you think a person running for president today would do this? Why or why not?

Getting the Main Idea

Why do you think Roosevelt is a role model for young people today?

Applying What You've Learned

Imagine that Roosevelt never had polio. Do you think he would have done his job as president differently? Why or why not?

Katharine Hathaway
Writer

Sometimes we forget that there is more than one kind of hero or **heroine.** We see the skills of sports stars on TV. Actors and actresses get their names in lights and their faces on the big screen. Books are written about those who are brave in wartime.

Katharine Hathaway was the kind of heroine whose story is not often told. Her deeds were not splashed across the front pages. Her courage was shown in her quiet **determination** to make a life for herself after a hard beginning.

A disease left her body disabled. Her artistic mind and spirit came through in her **autobiography,** *The Little Locksmith.*

"You must not miss it." —*New York Times*

THE LITTLE LOCKSMITH

A Memoir

Foreword by Alix Kates Shulman
Afterword by Nancy Mairs

KATHARINE BUTLER HATHAWAY

Katharine Hathaway

Katharine was born in 1890 in Salem, Massachusetts. Her family was educated and well off. She had two older brothers and later a younger sister. Katharine was a happy child, always laughing and playing.

When Katharine was five, she fell ill. She had **spinal tuberculosis.** Her family found a famous doctor to treat her. He treated Katharine with the very best methods of the day.

The goal was to keep Katharine's back straight. The doctor strapped her down tightly to a board. Her shoulders were tied down. Her head was pulled up off her chest by a leather halter. The halter was attached to a rope that went through a pulley at the head of the bed. On the end of the rope was a five-pound weight.

Katharine was held this way 24 hours a day. She could not move her head. She could not twist her body. She had to keep her back completely still and straight.

The purpose of all this was so Katharine would not get a twisted back. Her mother told her that she was lucky to have a famous doctor treat her. Otherwise, she might grow up to look like the "little locksmith."

The little locksmith was known as a **hunchback.** He came to their home to fix locks. Katharine had always loved to watch him work. His hands were so small and skillful as they fixed the locks.

He was a man, but he was the size of a child. On his back was a huge hump between his shoulders. He walked with a bobbing motion. In front, his chin was down on his chest.

As Katharine lay tied to her board, she watched the locksmith. She was glad that she would never look like that.

Even though Katharine was tied down, her hands and her mind were free. She held a pad of paper up in the air above her face and drew. She wrote letters and poems. She painted with watercolors. She made paper dolls. Katharine also spent many hours reading.

Katharine's room became the center of the home. Her brothers and sister spent many hours playing with her. Sometimes she felt as though she were the lucky one. She never had to pick up her clothes or go to school like the others.

Katharine learned to take pleasure in the smallest things. She learned to enjoy those things she could do and not worry about things she could not. So the days passed somewhat happily. But at night she suffered from terrible nightmares. The hours were long as she lay awake fearing to fall asleep and dream again.

When Katharine was 15, the treatment ended. After 10 years of lying down, she was allowed to stand up. She had to learn how to walk again. It took her days to get the courage to look in a mirror. She waited until she was alone to go to the mirror.

She said, "I didn't want anyone . . . to know how I felt when I saw myself for the first time. I just felt numb. That person in the mirror couldn't be me. I felt inside like a healthy . . . person. Oh, not like the one in the mirror! I had turned out after all like the little locksmith."

After 10 long years of suffering, she too had a hunched back. And she stood "no larger than a ten-year-old child." She couldn't understand how it had happened. She thought to herself that maybe "[an ugly] disguise had been cast over me, as if by a mean stepmother." She hoped that she might find a magic cure that would set her free.

While her body was disabled, her mind was not. It grew and grew, as her body could not.

Katharine's family treated her as they always had. Katharine knew that her family loved her and meant well. But she wished she had someone to talk to about her feelings. Instead she kept them all inside.

Katharine grew very close to her brother Warren. He was a student at Harvard. On weekends, he came home. He spent many hours talking with Katharine. Often he would take her for long buggy rides in the evening. It was a happy time for Katharine.

Full of joy, Katharine began writing poetry. Her poems were short. But they spoke of the joy of life. Writing the poems made her feel happy and peaceful. She showed her poems to her brother. He praised them. He told her she was a wonderful person. He said that she could know and feel great things. Katharine found great happiness in writing her poems. She felt as though she did have worth.

Warren made friends at Harvard. He began bringing some of them home on the weekends. When the young men met Katharine, they tried not to look at her. It was clear that they were bothered by her looks. They did not know what to say to her. So they paid no attention to her.

Katharine loved being with Warren and his friends. But she felt that she was "locked and hidden away in a prison where they could never see me or know that I was there; for I thought of myself as a [smart and happy] woman who was sitting in front of them . . . **deformed** and ashamed and shy."

She wrote, "I had known for a long time that nobody could ever fall in love with me, because of my being like the little locksmith." Year after year, Katharine watched others go ahead with their lives. Her brothers and sister left home. They married and had children. But Katharine still lived at home with her mother.

Katharine realized that there was no place for a disabled woman in her day and time. But she believed in herself. She set out to make a life for herself. In the end she built a life that went far beyond the role allowed her by society.

She went to Radcliffe College, a women's school. The girls there were free thinkers. They looked past Katharine's disability. They accepted her as the fine person she was. They thought of her as different and interesting. She made close friends.

Katharine began to come out of her shell. She made a place for herself among the artists and writers of the school. Katharine wrote poems, which were published in the Radcliffe literary magazine. Another was published in *The Atlantic Monthly.*

Katharine finished her degree at Radcliffe. She went home. She had decided that she would be a writer.

In 1921, she bought a house for herself on the coast of Maine. It was in the small village of Castine. The house stood by itself. It looked over the ocean. It was beautiful, but lonely. The house became a symbol of how she saw herself. She took great joy in fixing up the house. As she did so, she was changed herself.

The house brought her happiness. She wrote, "I believed that [everyone] could be happy. I believed that everyone should [go after happiness] boldly. I had been deprived of what is [thought of as] necessary for a happy life. I used all my wits to [get around] my fate, to make something out of nothing."

Visitors to the house loved it, too. One summer a painter from Japan came to visit. Katharine fell in love with him. It broke her heart when he moved to Paris. She left her house in Castine and moved to New York City. There she made many friends.

Katharine decided to go to Paris. There she was part of the thriving art scene of the 1920s. Some years later, she returned to the United States.

In 1932, at the age of 42, she married Daniel Hathaway. She sold her house in Castine. It reminded her of a sadder time in her life. She wanted a fresh start. The couple went back to Paris. Katharine wrote a book, *Mr. Muffet's Wonderful Cat and Her Trip to Paris.* With the money she made, the couple returned to the United States.

The Hathaways bought a home together in Blue Hill, Maine. There Katharine was content. She began writing *The Little Locksmith.* It was to be her finest work. She wrote the book as a "bread-and-butter [thank-you] letter to God." She said it was her "thanks for a lovely visit on the earth." She wrote to her brother that the book was "a little vase [holding] all that I have enjoyed."

The book told the story of how she made herself into an artist. It told how she gained her freedom from her disability. Katharine planned to follow it with many other books.

But Katharine's health had never been good. She hid the fact that she could never move or breathe easily. Her heart and lungs could not work well. They had been crushed all her life into her too-small chest. It got so bad that she could only breathe when curled up on her hands and knees. She died on the day before Christmas in 1942. She was 52 years old.

The Little Locksmith was published a year after her death. In 1946 a collection of her writings and drawings was published as *The Journals and Letters of the Little Locksmith.*

The Little Locksmith was a best-seller. But after it went out of print, it was forgotten. Years later, it was rediscovered. It has been called a "**classic** of early 20th-century **disability.**" It is a classic because so few writings about disabled women of that time exist.

Katharine Butler Hathaway was a woman of courage. She lived in a time that did not value women highly. People of her day thought women with disabilities had little worth. Yet Katharine believed in the value of her life. She made a place for herself in the world.

Remembering the Facts

1. What illness did Katharine have?

2. What disability did the "little locksmith" have?

3. How long was Katharine strapped to the board?

4. How did her brothers and sister help her?

5. What did she look like after the treatment was over?

6. How did the young men from Harvard treat Katharine?

7. Where did Katharine go to college?

8. What book was Katharine's finest work?

9. Why were Katharine's heart and lungs weak?

10. How old was Katharine when she married?

Understanding the Story

11. Katharine thought of her house in Castine as a symbol of her life. How do you think it was like her life?

12. In what ways do you think Katharine showed courage?

Getting the Main Idea

Why do you think Katharine Hathaway is a role model for young people?

Applying What You've Learned

There are many kinds of everyday heroes. These are people who give of themselves to help others in quiet ways. Give some examples.

Walt Disney
Cartoonist

The first sound **cartoon.** The first color cartoon. The first full-length cartoon movie. The most successful amusement park in history. A city of the future. Walt Disney is remembered for all these things and more. But most of all, he is loved for his character Mickey Mouse!

Walt Disney was born on December 5, 1901, in Chicago, Illinois. He was the fourth of five children. When he was five years old, the family moved to Marceline, Missouri. There his father bought a house and a 45-acre farm.

Walt Disney

The farm was a huge playground to Walt. He wandered all over the farm. He played in the mud. He herded pigs. He learned to watch for the animals living in the woods.

When Walt was six, he tried his hand at art for the first time. His parents had gone to town. Walt and his younger sister were left at home. Walt found a big bucket of tar. He thought it would make good paint. And the family's white house would make a great canvas. He began painting a picture of a nearby pig on the side of the house.

When his father came back, Walt was in big trouble. The tar would not come off. Walt's dad just left it on the house. Maybe that was why his father never approved of Walt's interest in art!

Walt's Aunt Maggie had more imagination. She brought paper and colored pencils to the house for Walt to use. Walt began hurrying through his farm chores so he would have time to draw. His drawings were very good.

Walt's mother taught him to read at home. When he was seven, he began school. Walt was not a good student. He was always finding things that interested him more than schoolwork. He just couldn't keep his mind on his work. His grades were poor. His teachers called him a "slow learner." They told his mother he would never be able to do much.

Two of Walt's older brothers did not like farm life. One day, they left home and moved to Kansas City. Now the job of running the farm fell on Walt's father alone. Walt and his brother Roy were still too young to do any heavy work.

Walt's father could not afford to pay men to help them on the farm. So, when Walt was eight, the farm had to be sold. The family moved to Kansas City.

Walt had only lived on the farm for four years. But he would remember it all his life. Later he used many of the animals and people from the farm in his cartoons.

Walt found the city exciting. Walt and his sister went back to school. His father bought a newspaper route with 700 customers. Walt and his older brother Roy had to get up at 3:30 each morning to deliver papers. This went on for six years. During all this time, Mr. Disney never paid the boys a penny for their work. He said they were paid in room and board.

When he finished his route, Walt went to school. He continued to be a poor student. Teachers complained that he did not pay attention. He failed to follow directions. It became clear that he could not do well with the usual classroom methods of teaching.

Walt tried harder in school. He told himself to pay attention. He wrote down what he was supposed to do. But he often wrote it down wrong and got the work wrong anyway. He did not think he was stupid. But his teachers told him over and over that he was slow. This did not make him feel very good about himself.

Even in drawing he could not please his teachers. One day the teacher told the class to draw a bowl of flowers that was sitting on her desk. Walt drew human faces on the flowers. And he put arms where the leaves were supposed to be! He got a low grade for not following directions.

In those days, anyone who got poor grades was called a slow learner. No one knew how to help these students. But some of them, like Walt Disney, learned how to help themselves when they got older.

When Walt Disney was growing up, no one had heard of learning disabilities. Years later, people could see that this was Walt's problem in school. But Walt had other things going for him. He was creative. And he was not afraid to try things over and over until he got them right.

Walt's best friend in school was Walter Pfeiffer. The Pfeiffer family loved shows and movies. Walt's father thought such things were a waste of time and money. So when the two boys started going to movies, Walt was careful not to let his father know.

The two boys began putting together their own shows. They used the jokes and songs they had heard in the movies they saw. One day the boys entered a contest at a nearby **theater.** Their play was called "Charlie Chaplin and the Count." They won fourth prize, which was 25 cents. (This was a lot in those days.) The boys made up other acts. Walt climbed out his bedroom window at night to go perform in the theater.

One day while delivering papers, Walt kicked a chunk of ice. A horseshoe nail went into his big toe. The wound took several weeks to heal. Walt got a rest from his paper route. This gave him time to think about his future. He knew he was a poor student. But he had been taking some art classes. He loved to draw cartoons. He decided that he would become a **cartoonist.** Walt's father told him that was a stupid idea. Walt did not listen.

When the United States entered World War I, Walt wanted to join the army. At 16 he was too young. But the Red Cross took **ambulance** drivers who were 17. Walt quit school. He lied about his age and signed up for the Red Cross. Soon he was on his way to France. The war had already ended by then. But drivers were still needed for many tasks. Walt ended up staying in France for a year.

Disney returned to the United States. But going back to high school was out of the question in his mind. He started looking for work. He landed a job with an ad company. He thought his **salary** was huge: $50 a month.

The job did not last long. Soon Walt had another job at Film Ad Company. The company made cartoon ads that were shown in movie theaters. Disney was excited about the job. Better yet, the salary was $40 a week. Disney was 19 years old and already making big money!

It was slow work making the early cartoons. First a figure was cut out of paper. It was then put on a background. A photo was taken. Then the position of the figure was changed a little. Another photo was taken. This process was repeated over and over. From this a simple kind of movement was shown on the screen. It did not look very real.

Disney thought there must be a better way. He studied and practiced. Finally he got an idea. He drew a picture of a boy standing in front of a ball. Then he drew another picture of the same boy with his leg raised a little. He drew more pictures, raising the leg more each time. Finally, the leg touched the ball. Next he drew pictures of the ball flying through the air. He photographed each of these pictures in turn with a movie camera. The end result was a scene with the boy kicking a ball. Walt Disney had found the secret of **animation.**

In 1923, Disney moved to Hollywood. He and his brother Roy became partners. Disney began making cartoons day and night. The first series was called "Alice in Cartoonland."

In 1927, Disney came up with a new cartoon star. It was a rabbit with long ears named Oswald. Oswald the Rabbit made Walt Disney famous. Soon Disney was turning out two or three cartoons a month.

Later that year, Disney had another idea for a cartoon. The star would be a mouse with big ears. Disney planned to name him

Mortimer Mouse. His wife Lilly told him Mortimer was not a good name for a mouse. She suggested the name Mickey.

The first two Mickey Mouse cartoons had no sound. When Warner Brothers came up with a way to make sound movies, Disney wanted to do his cartoons with sound. He made the cartoon "Steamboat Willie." The whole cartoon was based on sound. Mickey whistled on his way down the river. The ship's horn blasted. When the ship stopped at a farm, the animals added to the sounds. Walt Disney himself was the voice of Mickey.

Walt Disney had made the first sound cartoon in history. Mickey Mouse became a star! Soon Mickey was known around the world. Mickey's greatest role would come much later in a film called *Fantasia.*

Disney pushed ahead. He thought of new cartoon characters. Donald Duck. Minnie Mouse. Goofy. He never ran out of ideas. He was putting the energy and imagination that had driven his teachers crazy to good use.

In 1931, the first practical color film was invented. It was called Technicolor. Disney got two years' rights to use their film to make cartoons. "Flowers and Trees" was the first color cartoon. It was a huge hit. Walt Disney Studio won an Academy Award for the film that year. He won a second Academy Award that year! It was for Mickey Mouse. Disney soon had a hundred workers turning out two cartoons every two weeks.

The Disney studio grew. In 1937, the first **feature**-length cartoon was produced. It was *Snow White.* Other features followed. *Pinocchio, Bambi,* and *Fantasia* were a few of these.

Disney tried nature films. *Seal Island* (1948) had no people at all. It was a film about the life cycle of seals in Alaska. Many more films on wild animals were to follow.

Disney began making "family movies." Some of these were *Treasure Island* and *Mary Poppins.* These were exciting stories that often had lots of music.

In 1954, Disney tried television. *The Wonderful World of Disney* showed on Sunday evenings for many years. By the time of Disney's death, there were 330 hours of *Mickey Mouse Club* shows.

There were another 78 *Zorro* adventures. And there were 280 other Disney television shows.

In his lifetime, Disney produced 21 full-length animated films. He also did 493 short subjects, 47 live action films, and 7 true life adventures. It was an amazing output!

On July 18, 1957, Disney opened Disneyland. It has been the most successful amusement park in history. Disney got the idea for the park when he took his two small daughters to parks. He was not impressed with the parks. They were dirty and expensive. He made up his mind that some day he would build his own park. It would be clean and pretty. And it would be a place where the whole family could have fun together.

In 1965, Walt Disney was given the highest honor an American can get. President Johnson awarded him the **Presidential** Medal of Freedom. In the same year, he also won the Freedom Foundation Award.

In November of 1966, Disney went in for a checkup. He had a serious lung problem. On December 15, 1966, he died at the age of 65.

More Disney theme parks opened after Disney's death. In 1971, Walt Disney World Resort opened in Orlando, Florida. Since then, Disney parks have opened in Tokyo and Paris.

Another dream of Disney was to build a city of the future. This dream came true in 1982 when EPCOT Center was opened. Next, in Orlando, Disney-MGM Studios opened. Then came Animal Kingdom.

Today, the Disney business keeps growing. There are Disney movies. There are other types of films made by Touchstone Films. You can listen to a CD made by Hollywood Records. You can take a vacation on the Disney Cruise Line. You can buy Disney clothes or other goods. The Disney name is now a billion-dollar business.

Walt Disney created a vast empire. He won the respect of many. He won the top awards in show business. Everyone knew his name. But he will always be remembered most as the man who created Mickey Mouse.

Remembering the Facts

1. For which of his characters is Disney best loved?

2. What was the first thing Disney painted?

3. Why did Disney have trouble in school?

4. What work did Disney do for the Red Cross?

5. How were the first cartoons made?

6. What was the secret of animation?

7. What was the name of the first cartoon with sound?

8. What was the first color cartoon Disney made?

9. What was the first feature-length cartoon?

10. What was the most successful amusement park in history?

Understanding the Story

11. Why do you think Walt Disney quit high school?

12. Walt Disney once said, "A person should set his goal as early as he can. With enough effort, he may achieve it. Or he may find something else that is even more rewarding. But in the end—no matter what the outcome—he will know he has been alive." How do you think Disney lived up to these words?

Getting the Main Idea

Why do you think Walt Disney is a good role model for young people today?

Applying What You've Learned

Choose a simple action that can be easily drawn. Draw the pictures that would be needed to make a cartoon of that action. Show each step of the action.

Glenn Cunningham
Runner

He was known as "the world's fastest man." He was named **athlete** of the century. He set a world record for the one-mile run that stood for years. He was the greatest American miler of his time. Glenn Cunningham is still a hero to many of the world's runners.

Glenn Cunningham was born on August 4, 1909, in Atlanta, Kansas. His parents were farmers. Glenn had a brother Floyd, who was six years older.

The two boys attended a one-room school about a mile away. A wood-burning stove heated the school. In the

Glenn Cunningham

winter, the boys ran to school early to start the fire in the stove. For this, they each got a few pennies a day.

One day in the winter of 1916, the boys arrived at the cold school as usual. They filled the stove with wood. Floyd got the kerosene can. He poured the liquid onto the wood and struck a match.

This was the same thing the boys did every day. But a mistake had been made. Someone had used the school for a meeting the night before. They had lighted the room using gasoline lanterns. And the gasoline they had used in the lanterns had been poured into the empty kerosene can.

When Floyd lit the match, an explosion rocked the building. The room was quickly covered with flames.

Floyd was killed. Glenn's legs were badly burned. The doctor told Glenn's parents that if Glenn lived, his legs would have to be **amputated.** He did not hold out much hope that Glenn would live.

For the next six weeks, Glenn was between life and death. Finally he began to improve. He was in terrible pain. But slowly the burns began to heal. Glenn became more stable.

When Glenn looked at his legs, he was shocked. They were black and looked as if they'd been cooked. Most of the toes on the left foot had been burned off. The ball of his left foot was gone. The right leg was so scarred that he could not straighten it. It was now three inches shorter than the left leg. The doctors said that he would never walk again. It was the low point of Glenn's life.

Finally Glenn was able to go home from the hospital. He stayed in bed a long time. One day, his father brought home a pair of crutches. Glenn tried to use them, but the pain was too great. His father talked to him. "Never quit. Work your problems out," he said.

Glenn's parents spent hours rubbing his legs. They wanted to improve the blood **circulation.** They also stretched his legs and exercised them. In this way they hoped to build his muscles. There was no one to help them. They did it all themselves. When Glenn was stronger, he did the rubbing and exercises himself.

Glenn kept trying to use the crutches. It was painful putting weight on his legs. But Glenn was determined to walk again. He struggled for three years. Slowly he could put more and more weight on his legs.

When Glenn was 10 years old, he threw his crutches away. He still couldn't walk very well. But what he wanted to be able to do was run. Glenn later said, "I figured it out. It hurt like thunder to walk. But it didn't hurt at all when I ran. So for five or six years all I did was run."

The land around the Cunningham farm was a great place to run. For as far as the eye could see, the land was flat. Glenn began to run everywhere he went. His legs got stronger and stronger.

When Glenn was 12, he entered a one-mile race at the county fair. He won the race! The high school track coach was watching the race. He asked Glenn to join his team.

In high school Glenn was a hard worker. He did well in his studies. And he trained hard for the track team. He became the best miler in Kansas. In his third year of high school, the town took up a collection to send him to Chicago. There he entered the national high school meet. Glenn won the meet. And he set a record for the high school mile: 4 minutes and 24.7 seconds.

The track coach at the University of Kansas wanted Glenn on his team. Glenn was given a **scholarship.** The coach made a **prediction.** He said, "He could become the greatest miler America has ever had."

In 1931, Glenn set a new American record. He ran the mile in 4 minutes 11.1 seconds. In 1932 he won the NCAA 1,500-meter championship. But Glenn's old injuries were still a problem.

Glenn's ankles were very weak. He had blood circulation problems too. To prepare for each race, he had to **massage** his legs. Then he had to stretch his muscles. It took a long time to get ready. But Glenn learned how to work around these problems.

In 1932, Glenn **qualified** for the **Olympics.** He entered the 1,500-meter race. He set himself too fast a pace. He began to get tired too soon. He finished the race in fourth place. It was a big disappointment for him. But there would be other races.

In 1933, Glenn won the Sullivan Award. This is given each year to the most outstanding **amateur** athlete. He also won the NCAA mile. He won the AAU 800- and 1,500-meter runs. In 1934, he got his degree from the University of Kansas.

On June 16, 1934, Glenn ran his best race ever. It was a big meet at Princeton. As he was warming up, Glenn twisted his ankle. He almost fell. He sat down and started rubbing his ankle. When it was time for the race to start, Glenn was on his mark.

At first Glenn's ankle hurt. But soon he hit his stride. As the race went on, Glenn pulled out in front of the pack. He pulled farther and farther ahead. When the race ended, Glenn had set a new world record: 4 minutes, 6.7 seconds.

In 1936, Glenn again qualified for the Olympics. The Games were held in Berlin, Germany. Glenn won the silver medal in the 1,500-meter run.

Glenn went back to school. He got a Ph.D. in **physical education** in 1938. He kept on racing, too. At a race at Dartmouth College, he ran the mile in a stunning 4 minutes, 4.4 seconds. Newspapers around the world called him the "world's fastest man." *Newsweek* called him "the iron horse from Kansas."

Cunningham took a job as director of physical education at Cornell College in Iowa. He kept on racing until 1940. When World War II broke out, he joined the navy.

When the war ended, Cunningham left the navy. He knew that with his fame he could have his choice of jobs at many colleges. He could make a lot of money coaching track. But that was not what he wanted to do for the rest of his life. He and his wife Ruth bought a ranch in Kansas.

Glenn had become known as a speaker. He gave talks about overcoming your problems. Clubs, churches, and schools asked him to speak. He gave a strong "You can do it!" message to young people. After his talks, parents of kids with problems would come up to him to ask for advice. It wasn't long before he was saying, "Bring 'em out to the ranch for a while."

That was how it all started. The Cunninghams had more and more problem kids coming to stay with them. The couple decided that this was their calling in life. They named their ranch the Glenn Cunningham Youth Ranch. Over the years, nearly 10,000 children were sent to the Cunningham ranch. Some stayed for weeks until they could get back on their feet. Others stayed for years. The children lived and worked on the ranch with the Cunninghams' own 10 children.

The ranch was a great place. There were horses. There was a herd of bighorn sheep. There were monkeys, buffalo, goats, llamas, and peacocks.

There were rules to follow. Kids had to get up early and do chores. Each child had to help feed and water the animals. And every kid on the ranch was given a horse to take care of. Cunningham knew that hard work would take the children's minds off their problems. It would help their sense of worth. He knew that loving an animal could work wonders for a troubled child.

The ranch was always full of children. Sometimes things got wild. Cunningham's sense of humor kept things on an even keel. He told the kids, "Laughter builds strength in the soul. Without muscle in the soul you can't face the tough times in life."

Caring for so many children and running a ranch cost a lot of money. There were grocery bills and clothes for 35 kids. And the animals needed grain and hay.

For 30 years Cunningham traveled around the country on lecture tours to raise money for the ranch. He refused government aid. He did not want the government telling him how to run his ranch. The ranch made it on what Cunningham earned, plus money other people gave them.

In 1978, the Cunninghams closed the ranch and moved to town. They were out of money, and Ruth was ill. But it wasn't long before the ranch was open again. In June 1985, two young couples reopened the ranch. They wanted to continue the Cunningham's work. Glenn Cunningham again gave talks to raise money for the ranch.

Cunningham understood children who had lived through bad times. He had lived through as tough times as anyone. He taught the children to forget about the past and think about their futures.

He told the kids that weak areas could become strengths. He said, "Two men see a river. One sees it as a problem. The other sees it as a challenge. Guess who gets to the other side first."

On March 10, 1988, Glenn Cunningham died of a heart attack. He was doing chores on the ranch, the place he loved most.

Glenn Cunningham had left behind a fine legend as a runner. And he'd left an even finer one as a man.

Glenn Cunningham always said, "If you have a song in your heart, you owe the world a song." He spent his life giving of himself to help others. His life made a difference in the lives of thousands of children. No doubt he would think of that as his finest race ever.

Remembering the Facts

1. Where was Glenn Cunningham born?

2. How did Glenn's legs get badly burned?

3. What injuries were there to his left leg?

4. How long did he walk on crutches?

5. What was the first race Glenn won?

6. Where did Cunningham go to college?

7. What two Olympic Games did Cunningham run in?

8. What was the fastest time Cunningham ran the mile?

9. What was the purpose of the Youth Ranch?

10. How many children did the Cunninghams help?

Understanding the Story

11. Why do you think Cunningham was called "the iron horse from Kansas"?

12. Glenn Cunningham no longer holds the record for the fastest mile. Why do you think many runners still look at Cunningham as a role model?

Getting the Main Idea

Why do you think Glenn Cunningham is a good role model for young people?

Applying What You've Learned

Imagine that you are training as a runner. What kind of place would you choose to train in? Why?

Roy Campanella
Catcher

It was time for **physical therapy.** Miss Cole lined everyone up with their backs to the wall. She brought out a soft, white volleyball.

"Now," she said, "I'm going to teach you how to catch a ball."

Roy Campanella couldn't believe it. He thought, "It didn't hit me at first. I didn't get the full meaning of it all at once. But then it came to me. She was going to teach me how to catch a ball! It hit me like a [punch in the stomach]."

After all, Roy "Campy" Campanella was the famous catcher

Roy Campanella

of the Brooklyn Dodgers baseball team. Three times he had been named most valuable player in the National League. But now he was **paralyzed** from the shoulders down.

Campanella was stunned. "You're going to teach me to *catch?*" he asked.

Miss Cole caught her breath. She turned away. She wiped a tear from her eye. She realized what she had said.

But Campanella got control of himself. "OK," he said. "Let's go. This should be very interesting."

Softly Miss Cole threw the ball to Campanella. She threw it about chest high. She hoped he could catch it between his arms and wrists. But Campy couldn't raise his arms fast enough. The ball would hit him in the face or shoulders. Even worse, sometimes when he tried to catch it he would fall out of his wheelchair. Miss Cole would have to sit him back up again.

Campanella felt bad. The ball was so large. It was 10 times bigger than a baseball. But there was no way he could catch it! It was clear he was starting all over again. He knew then how tough his fight was going to be.

Roy Campanella was born on November 19, 1921, in Philadelphia, Pennsylvania. He was the youngest of four children.

Roy's mother was black. His father was Italian. Mr. Campanella sold vegetables from his truck. He got up at 5:00 A.M. to load his truck for the day. Roy helped him.

When Roy was 12, he got a milk route. He had to get up at 2:00 A.M. to deliver milk. He earned 25 cents a day. When he finished that, he helped his father load his truck. After school, he liked playing sports.

Roy's mother was very strict. Her children did their school-work. They minded their parents and teachers. And they always went to church on Sunday. There was never much money in the house, but it was a happy family.

The boys in Roy's neighborhood loved to play baseball. They would get up games in the schoolyard or the park. Few of the boys owned mitts. The balls were old and held together with black tape. The bats were held together with wire and tape. But that didn't matter. Roy could never get enough baseball.

Roy usually played catcher. He was a big boy and a leader. Those things seemed to go with being a catcher. Besides, no one else wanted to catch! And Roy was a great batter. He hit many long drives out of the park.

Being a catcher without the right equipment is a dangerous job. Roy had no mitt. He had no face guard. He had no pads to protect his chest. Many times he came home with bruises and sprains in his hands. One time a ball smashed his nose. He tried to hide his **injuries** from his parents. But it didn't always work.

After a while, Roy's father had had enough. He told Roy to stop playing ball. Roy was so upset, his father finally changed his mind. Roy promised to be more careful.

By the time Roy was 14 years old, he was an excellent ball-player. He was asked to catch for an American Legion team. He was the only black player on the team. In those days, black and white athletes did not play sports together.

The next year, when Roy was 15, he was again playing for the American Legion team. After the game, a man came up to him. It was Tom Dixon, catcher for the Bacharach Giants, a black pro baseball team.

Dixon asked Roy to play for the team. They would be going out of town to play some games that very weekend. Roy told them he didn't think his parents would let him go. They still weren't too happy about his ball playing.

Dixon talked to Roy's parents. Finally, they worked out a deal. Roy could go. But Dixon was to see that Roy went to church on Sunday. Roy would earn $35 for the weekend.

While he was playing with the Giants, Roy was spotted by the manager of the Baltimore Elites. The Elites were part of the Negro National League. Roy, at 15, would earn regular pay for the summer.

Roy loved the life of a ballplayer. He liked riding around the country in a bus. The team stayed in old hotels and ate poor meals. But none of this bothered Roy. He was in a new town each day. And he was playing ball in the black **major leagues.** He didn't think life could get much better!

The Elites' star catcher, "Biz" Mackey, liked Roy. He spent many hours coaching him. Roy learned to throw fast. And he could throw the ball just where he wanted it. Base runners were afraid to try to steal a base. Roy learned to study his pitchers and learned to work with them. He also studied the hitters to learn their weaknesses.

Roy had a lot to learn. Being a catcher is not an easy job. The catcher is the only one who can see all the other players. Often he runs the **defense** of the team. On each pitch, he tells the pitcher what kind of ball to throw. He often has to move quickly to catch every ball. And he always has to be ready to throw the ball to put out a base runner.

When the summer was over, Roy returned to school. But he was no longer allowed to play high school ball. Some schools said he had become a pro. Roy turned 16 that fall. He and his parents agreed he could quit school to play baseball. Roy left home for his first full season with the Elites.

Roy was thrilled. He was playing in the same league as his hero, Josh Gibson! Gibson took a liking to Roy. He worked with him, giving him tips on batting and catching. By the next season, Roy was first-string catcher.

Players for the Negro National League were not paid well. In the winters, Roy and many others played ball in Puerto Rico, Cuba, and Mexico. Roy has said that during these years he played 220 games a year. He played ball for all but two weeks of the year. One time he was catcher in two doubleheaders in one day (four games)!

For seven years Roy kept up this schedule of play. Summers with the Elites. Winter ball in Puerto Rico. Roy became known as a hard worker and a good player. In 1939, Roy and the Elites were the champions of the Negro League. Also in 1939, Roy married Ruthe Willis. They later had five children.

In those days, the Negro National League was as high as a black player could go. There were some great black players. Some of these were Satchel Paige, Josh Gibson, and Jackie Robinson. But all were paid far less than white players.

Many black players wanted to play in the white major leagues. No one thought it would ever happen. But suddenly, it did! Branch Rickey was the owner of the Brooklyn Dodgers. He thought black players should be given the chance to play on any team if they were good enough. On October 23, 1945, the Dodgers signed Jackie Robinson. He was the first black player in the white major leagues.

In 1946, Rickey asked Roy to join the Dodgers. He agreed. He played his first season with a farm club in Nashua, New Hampshire.

That year, the Nashua farm team won the **pennant** for their league. Roy had made 13 home runs. He was named the most valuable player of the league.

The next season, Roy was moved to Montreal. This was the Dodgers' top farm club. Again, he won the most valuable player award.

In 1948, Roy was called up to the Brooklyn Dodgers. The team was in a slump. They were in last place in the league. The day Roy arrived, he hit a double and two singles. The next day, he hit two home runs and a single. The Dodgers began to win their games. By the end of the season, they were in third place.

All through 1949, the Dodgers won games. They won the National League pennant. But the Yankees won the World Series. Still, Roy had played well. He had made no errors. And he had made a home run and three other hits. He was on his way to fame!

In 1950, Roy had a great year. He had the best record of all major league catchers. And he hit 31 home runs. He topped this in 1951, hitting 33 home runs. He batted in 108 other runs. His batting average was .325.

Roy had many injuries from his playing. He broke his right thumb. Then he was spiked on the hand. Next he hurt his elbow in a crash at home plate. He was hit in the head by a ball. Then he pulled a muscle in his leg. He kept right on playing. Even with all the injuries, he was named MVP in 1951.

1952 was another year for injuries. But Roy hit well enough to help the Dodgers win the pennant again. They still couldn't beat the powerful Yankees in the World Series.

Roy had a great year in 1953. He set three records for catchers. First, he hit 42 home runs. He led the league with 142 runs batted in. And he put out 807 base runners. For the second time, Roy was named MVP of the National League. But once again, the Yankees took the World Series.

The next year Roy was again troubled by injuries. He had nerve damage in his left hand. He had two operations.

But in 1955, Roy came back strong. Once again, the Dodgers won the pennant. For the fifth year, they faced the Yankees in the World Series. Each team won three games. The Series was tied. The winner would be decided in the seventh game. Roy's hitting helped win the game for the Dodgers! The fans went wild. At last, the Dodgers had become world champs. Roy Campanella was voted MVP for the third time in five years.

The next two years were hard for Roy. His hands hurt all the time. He had more operations. Batting and catching became painful. But with all this, he kept on playing. He was still a star player.

But with no warning, his playing days ended. On January 28, 1958, Roy's car crashed on an icy road. Roy broke his neck. He nearly lost his life as well. Roy was paralyzed from the shoulders down. He could barely move his arms. He would be in a wheelchair the rest of his life.

Roy refused to give up. He worked hard to get back his strength. He worked hard with his physical therapist Miss Cole. He learned how to get around. He learned to take care of himself. And he returned to his great love—baseball.

In 1959, when spring training began, Roy took a coaching job with the Dodgers. He coached the catching team. He had a lot of knowledge to share with the young catchers. He passed along the many tips he had learned over the years.

When the 1959 season started, the Dodgers and the Yankees played an **exhibition** game in Roy's honor. The largest crowd in the history of baseball was there. Roy was wheeled onto the field before the game. He threw out the opening ball! The crowd began to cheer. The cheering went on and on. The Dodgers retired Roy's number. No player on that team would ever wear 39 again.

Roy continued to coach for the Dodgers. He worked as a television **commentator.** In 1969, he was named to the Baseball Hall of Fame. One way or another, Roy would always be a part of baseball.

Roy "Campy" Campanella died at his home on June 26, 1993. He will be remembered as one of the greatest catchers in baseball. But he will also be remembered for refusing to give up. Roy was a man of great faith and courage.

Roy lived his life to the fullest, even when he became disabled. He became stronger in spirit than before. He is an example to all of us. Roy lived the title of his **autobiography,** *It's Good to Be Alive!*

Remembering the Facts

1. How did Roy first earn money as a boy?

2. Why did Roy often get hurt playing ball as a boy?

3. What was the first pro black team Roy played for?

4. What kind of team was the Baltimore Elites?

5. Why did many black players play winter ball in Puerto Rico?

6. What National League team did Roy play for?

7. In what three years was Roy named MVP in the National League?

8. Which team did the Dodgers beat to win the 1955 World Series?

9. How did the Dodgers honor Roy after his accident?

10. Name a job Roy did after his accident.

Understanding the Story

11. Roy's autobiography, *It's Good to Be Alive,* was written in 1959. This was not long after his accident. What do you think the title says about the man?

12. In what ways did Roy show a strong spirit before the accident?

Getting the Main Idea

How do you think Roy Campanella is a good role model for young people today?

Applying What You've Learned

Imagine that you are a pro football player who has become disabled. What do you think would be some ways you could still contribute to your sport?

Bernard Bragg
Actor

There were ten 13-year-old boys in the class. All of them were deaf. They were students at the New York School for the Deaf.

The boys were always making noise. Stamping their feet on the floor. Dropping books. Drumming their fingers. Or making the chalk squeak on the board. Of course, being deaf, they didn't know how noisy they were. But it drove their teacher, Mr. Ryder, crazy. What he hated the most was the sound of their loud laughter.

Bernard Bragg

One day, Mr. Ryder had had enough. He told the class he was going to teach them how to laugh. He had the boys stand up and put their hands on their ribs. They breathed in, then let the air out. While they did, they were to say "aaah," "aaah . . .". When they finally made the sound he wanted, he patted them on the head.

One of the boys, Bernard, never forgot these lessons. Nearly 50 years later, when he was a world-famous actor, Bernard wrote his **autobiography.** He called it *Lessons in Laughter.*

Bernard Bragg was born on September 27, 1928. He was born deaf. His parents were both deaf, too.

Bernard and his parents talked to each other using sign language. Bernard loved watching his mother's hands as she told him stories. And his father signed wonderful tales of knights and princes to his young son.

As a young child, Bernard did not know he was deaf. After all, he was just like everyone else around him. His parents had many deaf friends. They would often come to the Bragg house to play cards or talk. They talked using sign language.

Bernard's father was an actor and **mime.** He led a group of deaf actors. Bernard loved to watch his father's acting company. He would stand in the **wings** of the stage. Sometimes, if there was a part for a young child, Bernard got the job. His love for the stage began.

Bernard loved to watch movies, too. Charlie Chaplin, Mae West, and Charlie Chan were his favorite stars. It wasn't long before he was **imitating** these actors in his living room. Everyone was amazed by how good he was!

As he grew older, Bernard learned that he was different from other people. He couldn't understand why some people moved their mouths instead of talking with their hands. His mother tried to explain that he was deaf, and they could hear. That didn't make any sense to Bernard.

One morning, his mother woke him up early. They left the apartment and went across town to a large old building. It was then that Bernard's mother told him, "You're going to school." Bernard was not sure what school was. But he saw that his mother planned to leave him there. He was not at all happy!

After his mother left, Bernard was given a uniform to put on. Next he was taken to the playroom. Other deaf children were playing there. Bernard had never seen another deaf child. It wasn't long before the children were signing to each other. Bernard was glad he could talk to the others. But he was lonely being away from home.

The school Bernard went to was the New York School for the Deaf. The teachers taught the students to talk and to **lip-read.** The children in the class wore **headphones.** These were hooked up to an **amplifier** on the teacher's desk. This would make the sounds of speech louder. If children had any hearing left, they would be able to learn speech better this way. But Bernard had no hearing at all. So this method did not help him.

Bernard had to try to learn to speak by watching the position of the teacher's mouth. He put his hand on her throat or cheek to feel the **vibration.** Slowly, he learned to make the sounds of the letters. He worked on this all the years he was in school. But he was never able to speak clearly. People could not understand him.

In each class, the teachers talked to the students as if they could hear. They did not use signs. Bernard had to try to understand what they were saying by reading their lips. This was not easy at all! He understood very little of what was being said.

Bernard worked hard in school. He learned to read books and to write good sentences. Writing well is hard to do for a person born deaf. Learning the names of things is not hard. But learning to put words together correctly to make sentences is hard.

When Bernard was 17, a new English teacher came to the school. Mr. Panara made his students love to learn. When he found out that Bernard was interested in acting, he said they could put on a play for the school. The play they chose was *The Christmas Bell.* Bernard played the lead role. He did a wonderful job.

The next year they did a longer play: *A Christmas Carol.* Bernard played Scrooge. Everyone was amazed at Bernard's acting skill. Mr. Panara knew Bernard could have a great future as an actor.

Bernard finished high school at the top of his class. The next year he entered Gallaudet College. This school is the only university for the deaf in the United States. It was begun in 1864. The president of the United States signs every **diploma** given out.

After Bernard's first year in college, he applied for a summer job as a dishwasher at a camp. When he went for the **interview,** he told the man that he was deaf. The man pointed to a door. Bernard opened it and went through. He was out on the street.

Bernard was angry. He knew the man didn't want to hire him because he was deaf. He went back into the man's office. He wrote down what he wanted. The man was surprised to see how well Bernard could write. Bernard got the job.

When Bernard returned to college, he decided to **major** in English **literature.** He played the lead roles in three plays. He directed another play. Bernard worked hard in school. But he loved what he was doing.

In June 1952, Bernard got his college degree. He was hired to teach by the California School for the Deaf. This was one of the best schools for the deaf in the United States. The school rarely hired teachers who had no experience. But they wanted Bernard. He would teach there for the next 15 years.

Bragg was pleased to have such a fine job. But he really didn't want to teach at all. He wanted to be an actor. This was not a very practical goal. No deaf people made a living by acting at that time.

However, Bragg found teaching fun. He taught all the sixth grade subjects. When he could, he used acting in his classroom. He started an acting club. They put on one play per year. Bragg enjoyed this, but it was not enough for him.

One day, Bragg saw a story about Marcel Marceau. Marceau was a famous French mime. In mime, a story is told without words. Only actions show what is happening. Marceau was coming to San Francisco to do a show. Bragg took the day off and went to see him. Bragg loved what he saw. Here was a way to reach all people, hearing and deaf. He knew he had to talk to Marceau!

Bragg went **backstage.** He told Marceau that he was deaf. He wanted to know where he could go to study mime. Marceau asked Bragg to show him what he could do. Bragg did a mime about Noah's Ark. He played all the animals, one after another. Then he did a mime about a band. He acted out each instrument in turn. Then he played the **conductor.** Marceau was amazed! He asked Bragg to come to Paris to study with him that summer. Bragg said "yes" right away.

Bragg's parents were not happy about his decision. They thought there was no future in acting. They wanted Bragg to stick to teaching, or to learn a good trade.

But Bragg wouldn't listen to them. The theater was all he wanted. He would go to Paris! It didn't matter that he had no money. He borrowed and saved until he had enough. On June 4, 1956, Bragg flew to Paris.

Marcel Marceau was known the world over. He and a company of seven players did nightly shows at a Paris theater. Bragg learned many things from him. He improved his acts. It was not long before he was joining in the show.

At the end of the summer, Bragg sailed back to the United States. Word spread that the deaf schoolteacher had studied with Marcel Marceau. The ship's captain told the press about his passenger. So Bragg's parents saw their son on the TV news before he got home.

Bragg returned to the California School for the Deaf. He started teaching again. He also kept doing mime. One day he did his act in a nightclub. Someone took pictures of him and sent them to *Parade* magazine.

A club in San Francisco called Back Stage saw the story. They called and asked him to perform there. While he was working there, *Life* magazine reporters visited the club. They liked what they saw. Bernard was named one of the best small nightclub performers for that year. Bragg worked at Back Stage until March 1958.

The next summer, Bragg did his one-man show in clubs all over Los Angeles. His show, "An Evening with the Mask," won praise.

Bragg got his own TV show. It was a half-hour children's show called "The Quiet Man." In it he mimed many well-loved children's stories. He played every part himself.

The summer of 1962, Bragg toured Europe. Everywhere he went, people loved him. He was known as "America's Master of Mime."

In 1967, the founder of the first professional deaf theater company asked Bragg to help organize the group. This had long been a dream of his. The group would be called the National Theater of the Deaf (NTD). Bragg quit teaching to work on the NTD. It was a chance for deaf actors to perform for both hearing and deaf worlds. His goal was to teach people about deafness.

The first group of NTD actors came together in August 1967. There were fourteen deaf actors and three hearing **narrators.** The actors used "sign-mime." Signs and mime were put together to tell a story. Audiences loved the graceful, beautiful performances. As the deaf actors signed, the hearing narrators spoke aloud what was being said. The beauty of the language of signs was clear to all.

In the fall of 1968, the Little Theater of the Deaf was begun. It was directed toward children.They hoped to help children understand deaf people.

On February 24, 1969, the NTD opened on Broadway. The deaf actors were thrilled. Their company had been together only 18 months. And they had already made it big!

In the spring of 1969, the NTD went on a tour of Europe. They met deaf people wherever they went. They saw the only other deaf theater group in the world: The Russian Theater of the Deaf. Later, Bragg spent six weeks in Russia as an artist-in-**residence.**

Bragg worked with the NTD for ten years. In 1977, he decided to try other things. He wanted to work by himself. That year Bragg did a world tour of 38 cities. He gave lectures and did mime and poetry for his audiences.

Bragg kept on performing. He wrote and directed plays, too. Most of his work is about the world of the deaf. All of it is in sign language.

Bragg has earned many awards. The World Federation of the Deaf honored him. He was given the International Merit Award for his work with deaf actors around the world. Gallaudet awarded him an honorary **doctorate** in 1988. He has been artist-in-residence at many colleges, including Harvard.

In 1998, Bragg gave money to Gallaudet University. The money will be used to set up an **endowed chair.** A "chair" is a special kind of job for a gifted person. Deaf artists or scholars will be appointed to the chair for a two- or three-year term. While in the chair, they must write a play, story, or poems about deaf people.

This way, Bragg can be sure that people will be writing about deaf people for many years to come. Bragg has made sure that the story of the deaf is not forgotten, even after he is gone.

Remembering the Facts

1. Why did Bernard not know that he was deaf for so long?

2. What was Bernard's introduction to theater?

3. Why is it so hard for a child born deaf to learn to talk well?

4. Why is it hard for deaf children to learn to write well?

5. Where did Bernard go to college?

6. At which school did Bragg teach?

7. Who was the famous mime Bragg studied with in Paris?

8. What was the theater group Bragg helped start?

9. What work did Bragg do when he left the theater group?

10. What gift did Bragg give to Gallaudet University in 1998?

Understanding the Story

11. Why do you think Bragg was turned down for the dishwashing job?

12. In what ways do you think Bragg's gift to Gallaudet will help the deaf?

Getting the Main Idea

Why do you think Bernard Bragg is a good role model for young people?

Applying What You've Learned

Imagine that you suddenly go deaf. Make a list of ways this would change your life.

Ray Charles
Musician

Ray Charles is a national treasure. He is known as the "**genius of soul.**" For 50 years he has thrilled people of all ages with his music.

Ray Charles is a singer. He plays the piano. He writes and arranges music. He has blended **jazz, blues, gospel,** and pop music to make his own sound called "soul." Fans around the world love him.

Ray Charles was born in Albany, Georgia on September 23, 1930. A few months later, his family moved to Greenville, Florida. It was a tiny country town.

Ray Charles

They were poor. As Ray put it, "We were on the bottom of the ladder looking up at everyone else. Nothing below us 'cept the ground." Ray was seven years old when he got his first pair of shoes.

Ray rarely saw his father. His mother, who was 15 when he was born, raised him. She had quit school after fifth grade. She earned a living washing and ironing clothes. When Ray was a year old, his brother George was born.

Ray's mother believed in being strict. By the time the boys were five and four, she had them working hard doing chores. On Sunday they always went to church. Ray loved the singing.

Ray loved music from an early age. In his **autobiography,** he said, "I was born with music inside me. Music was one of my parts. Like my ribs, my liver, my kidneys, my heart. Like my blood. It was already a force within me when I arrived on the scene. It was a need for me—like food or water."

Down the road from Ray lived Mr. Pit. He owned the Red Wing Café. It was the center of the black community. Mr. Pit had a jukebox and an old beat-up piano. But he could play that old piano like a master.

From the age of three, Ray spent hours at the Café. He watched his neighbor Mr. Pit play. And he tried to play himself. Ray also loved to listen to blues and **boogie-woogie** on the jukebox.

One day Ray and his four-year-old brother George were playing outside. In the backyard his mother kept four large tubs she used for washing clothes. The boys liked to swim in the tub that was filled with rinse water.

George climbed into the tub to swim. He began to yell and kick. At first Ray thought he was playing. Soon he realized his brother was in trouble. He tried to pull him out. But he wasn't strong enough to do it. So he ran for his mother. But it was too late. His brother was dead. It was an awful thing for Ray to have seen. And it turned out to be one of the last things he would ever see.

Over the next two years, Ray slowly lost his sight. His mother took him to many doctors. But there was nothing they could do. By the time Ray was seven, he was totally blind.

There was no school for a blind child in Greenville. Ray would have to go to the Florida State School for the Deaf and the Blind. It was 160 miles away in St. Augustine, Florida. In September, Ray left for school on the train. He was seven years old and all by himself. He cried for weeks. But finally he made up his mind to get used to it.

First, Ray learned **braille.** (Braille is a way for the blind to read. Raised dots stand for letters and numbers. Blind people read them by touch.) Math and music were his favorite subjects. There was a woodworking shop at the school. There he learned how to carve. He learned how to weave cane bottoms for chairs. He became very good at making baskets. He also made brooms and mops.

Ray also got his first formal piano lessons. He took to it right away. But he wasn't allowed to play the blues at school. He could play only **classical** music. Soon he had jobs playing for ladies at tea parties in St. Augustine.

Already, at the age of eight, piano was very important to Ray. He said, "When I was a kid, I never thought about being famous or rich. But I did think about being great. I wanted to be a great musician."

Ray began playing in bands at school. He wanted to write his own music. By the time he was 14, Ray had learned to write for the entire band. He could write all the parts and make them blend. He just called out the notes to someone else to write down. First one part, then the next. This is how he still writes music today. He does it all in his head.

When Ray was 15, his mother died. He decided to quit school. Ray thought he could make a living as a musician. And there was no one to tell him "no."

Ray moved to Jacksonville, Florida. He took any jobs he could get. He played whatever music he was asked for. He played at all the roughest clubs. He learned from the other musicians, who were all older. He improved his playing by "stealing any lick that wasn't nailed down." (That meant he copied what the others were doing.)

It was no picnic for young Ray. He often had no place to live. And there were times he almost starved. When he had no work, he hung around local musician's hangouts.

After a year, he moved on to Orlando. He stayed there another year before moving to Tampa. One day Ray decided he'd like to see more of the country. He went to Seattle. That was about as far away from Florida as you could get. Seattle was a turning point in Ray's life. There he became popular in nightclubs.

Ray and two friends formed the McSon Trio. They recorded some records. One of Ray's tunes was called "Baby, Let Me Hold Your Hand." This was his first national hit. In 1948, the group became the first black group to have a sponsored TV show in the northwest.

Ray decided he needed a catchy name. He had been born Ray Charles Robinson. He dropped the Robinson and became Ray Charles. (He didn't want to be Ray Robinson because there was a famous black boxer named "Sugar" Ray Robinson.)

In 1950, Ray moved to Los Angeles. There he played all kinds of music: blues, jazz, or just popular songs.

Soon after that, he went on the road. He traveled across the South. It was called the "chitlin' circuit." This meant he played in a lot of clubs that were mainly for black people. As a black singer, he was not welcome in white clubs in the South.

Ray had grown up with **segregation.** At the Florida School for the Deaf and the Blind, segregation was the rule. This was true for both the deaf and the blind children. Even as a child, Ray found this silly. The blind children couldn't even see each other to tell who was what color.

Ray later said, "I knew that being blind was suddenly an aid. I never learned to stop at the skin. If I looked at a man or a woman, I wanted to see inside. (Worrying about) color is stupid. It gets in the way. It's something I just can't see."

Still, on the road in the 1950s, Ray ran into a number of problems because of segregation.

Ray was on the road all the time. When he wasn't on the road, he was recording. By the time he was 24, he had recorded 40 singles. In 1953, he arranged and played piano on "The Things I Used to Do." This record sold a million copies.

In the 1950s, Ray began creating a new sound. With just one song, "I Got a Woman," he changed the world of music forever! This song unleashed a new sound called "soul." "I Got a Woman" was an old gospel song. Ray turned it into a rhythm and blues number. Then he sang it with the passion of gospel music. Soul was born! Soul combined gospel music with rhythm and blues.

He signed a contract with Atlantic records. He had three big records: "A Fool for You," "Drown in My Own Tears," and "Hallelujah, I Love Her So." In 1959, he made the top of the pop charts. The song was "What'd I Say."

In 1960, Ray made his first European tour. It was a huge success. Every year since then (except for one) he has toured Europe again.

Ray began recording for ABC/Paramount Records in 1960. The first song he recorded with them was "Georgia on My Mind." (Ray had done his own arrangement of the old Hoagie Carmichel tune.) This became his biggest hit of all time. In fact, it later became the state song of Georgia. In 1962, Ray sold $8 million worth of records. This was a lot for that time!

Ray was making lots of money. In 1962, he had his own recording studio built in Los Angeles. It was called RPM International.

Ray loved all kinds of music. He even did country and western singing. In 1962, he recorded the country classic "I Can't Stop Loving You." He kept on doing a variety of kinds of music. Pop hits. Broadway songs. Blues. Gospel. Jazz. Ray did them all.

Because Ray did it so well, the blues (which had once been enjoyed only by black audiences) increased in popularity. Ray made jazz popular with many more people. Country and western music got a boost from Ray. And Ray Charles was even a part of the invention of rock 'n' roll!

In 1966, Thomas Thompson wrote about Ray for *Life* magazine. He said, "His [place in music] is hard to define. The best blues singer around? Of course, but don't stop there. He is also the best singer of jazz, of gospel, of country and western. He has drawn from each of these musical streams. He has made a river which he alone can travel."

The lifestyle of a singer can be hard. Ray began using drugs. He was arrested several times. Finally, he knew he had to stop. At 35, he quit "cold turkey." (Cold turkey means that he just decided to stop and did it.) He never returned to his drug habit.

During the Civil Rights movement of the 1960s, Ray supported Dr. Martin Luther King. The two were good friends. Ray raised lots of money to support the movement.

Ray played in concerts and on TV around the world. In the 1970s, he created his own label. It was called Crossover. By the 1980s, he had over 70 top singles.

Ray had become a living legend. Many famous musicians said they had learned from him. Even the Beatles said he had **inspired** them.

To this day, he writes and arranges his own music. He pays no attention to what is popular. He says that he "**gleans** from the attic of my mind" what sounds right.

In 1986, President Reagan awarded Ray the Presidential Medal of Freedom. That same year he was voted into the Rock 'n' Roll Hall of Fame. In 1988, he won the Grammy Lifetime Achievement Award.

Ray had a part in the movie *The Blues Brothers.* He has acted in television shows. PBS did a film on his life called *The Genius of Soul.* Later Fox did a film of his life called *50 Years of Music Making.*

In January 1993, Ray sang "America the Beautiful" for President Clinton's **inaugural** ceremony at the Lincoln Memorial. Later that year, Clinton awarded him the National Medal of Arts.

Ray had always wanted to be great. He has reached his goal. He is one of the greats of twentieth-century music. His music has touched millions of people around the world.

His greatness began with the talent he had at birth. But it grew because of his long hours of work to perfect it. He soaked up the styles and sounds of his time. Then he made his own special sound. His voice is one of a kind.

To Ray, blindness was not a handicap. In his autobiography, Ray said, "There were three things I never wanted to own when I was a kid. A dog. A cane. And a guitar. In my brain, they each meant blindness and helplessness. . . . I didn't want to depend on anyone or anything other than myself." Ray Charles has made it. And in doing so, he has brought light into the darkness for millions.

Remembering the Facts

1. What is Ray Charles known as?

2. Where did Ray grow up?

3. Who first taught Ray to play the piano?

4. How old was Ray when he lost his sight?

5. Where did Ray go to school?

6. How does Ray write music?

7. What was Ray's first national hit?

8. Ray's recording of what song is the state song of Georgia?

9. What award did President Reagan give Ray?

10. What is the name for the kind of music Ray sings most?

Understanding the Story

11. Why is it clear that Ray had a talent from birth?

12. Why do you think Ray played mostly for black audiences in the 1950s?

Getting the Main Idea

Why do you think Ray Charles is a good role model for young people today?

Applying What You've Learned

Imagine that Ray Charles had been born white and middle class and had his sight. Do you think that would have made a difference in his music? Why or why not? Give reasons for your answer.

Arthur Ashe
Tennis Player

Many people look up to **athletes** because of their skill in their sport. They often don't think about what kind of person the athlete is. Some athletes deserve to be role models. Others do not.

Arthur Ashe

Arthur Ashe won fame on the tennis court. He won 51 titles in tennis. An African-American athlete, he broke one **racial barrier** after another. But it is the things he did off the court that made him a hero.

Ashe used his fame as a way to fight for just causes. He worked for justice for black people. He worked for heart disease **research.** And he fought hard against AIDS.

Ashe was a great athlete. But this was not enough for him. He wanted to be a great human being. In his book, *Days of Grace,* he said, "I know I could never forgive myself if I . . . lived without [a good] purpose. [I could not live] without trying to help the poor and unfortunate. . . . Perhaps the real joy in life comes with trying to help others."

Arthur Ashe was born on July 10, 1943, in Richmond, Virginia. Arthur's mother taught him to read and love books. His father taught him the value of hard work. Arthur's father was always working. He was a gardener and carpenter for some rich white families in town. He cooked and waited on tables for them too.

Richmond, like other cities in the South at that time, was **segregated.** There were laws to keep blacks and whites apart. Arthur had to learn to live with this. It was the law. Arthur went to an all-black school. He played in parks that were for blacks. He drank from water fountains for blacks. And he rode at the back of the bus. That was how things were for black people in those days.

At this time, Arthur's father was the manager of Brookfield Park. The park had a pool, baseball fields, and tennis courts. Best of all, the Ashes got to live in a small house right in the park. What a break for a boy who loved sports!

When Arthur was six, his mother died. Arthur and his younger brother were raised by their father. But Arthur never forgot his mother's teachings.

Arthur wanted to be a football player. But he was thin and weak. He decided he might like to learn to play tennis.

Richmond's top black tennis player, Ron Charity, practiced at the park. Arthur often stood and watched him. One day, Charity turned to Arthur. "Would you like to learn to play?" he asked.

"Yes, I would," Arthur answered. His life would never be the same. Over the next two years, Charity taught Arthur. Arthur was a quick learner. By the time Arthur was 10, people were calling him "the kid who could play tennis."

In 1953, Charity introduced Arthur to Dr. Robert W. Johnson. Dr. Johnson, a tennis player himself, helped young black tennis players. In the summers, he invited them to his home. He coached them. He entered them in **tournaments.**

Dr. Johnson coached Arthur for eight summers. When Arthur was 12, he was ranked number one in the United States for his age group. He won many tournaments. At 14, he traveled to Maryland. He was the first black athlete to play in the Maryland state tournament. When he was 17, Arthur won the American

Tennis Association junior title. He won the men's title too. He was the youngest person ever to win the men's title.

Because he was black, Arthur was not allowed to enter most tournaments in the South. He had to travel to states that allowed black athletes to play. His senior year in high school, Arthur moved to St. Louis. There he could enter any tournament he chose.

In 1960, Arthur won the National Junior Indoor title. He graduated first in his high school class. Then he won a tennis **scholarship** to UCLA. He was the first African American to be offered a scholarship there. Also that year, he appeared in *Sports Illustrated* for the first time.

Ashe was excited to learn that Pancho Gonzales lived only a few blocks from UCLA. Gonzales was one of the best tennis players in the world. He had faced some of the same problems as Ashe had because he was Mexican American. The two practiced together. Ashe's game got better and better.

Ashe played a lot of tennis in college. He won the NCAA singles and doubles titles. He led UCLA to a team championship. And, he got his degree in business in 1966.

In 1963, Ashe played at Wimbledon. He did not win. But his playing attracted attention. He was the first African American to be chosen for the U.S. Davis Cup team. This team played against other countries. He played on this team from 1963 to 1970.

By now, Ashe was famous. He made the cover of *Sports Illustrated* and *Life* magazines. He appeared in ads for soft drinks. His name was printed on tennis rackets. Everyone knew his name.

Ashe used his fame to help others. These were the days of the civil rights movement in the United States. Ashe talked about civil rights on TV and in newspapers. He also spoke out against **injustice** toward black people.

In 1968, Ashe won the U.S. Open men's singles titles. He helped win the Davis Cup for the United States. He was the first black player to win both titles. Now Ashe was ranked the number one player in the United States.

Ashe helped start the USTA National Junior Tennis League. This program was to help inner-city tennis players. Most were black and did not often get the chance to play tennis.

Ashe was unhappy about injustices he saw in South Africa. In the 1970s, South Africa still had segregation laws. (This had been made against the law in the United States in 1954.) People all over the world opposed these laws. They did not want to have anything to do with South Africa.

Ashe wanted to travel to South Africa. He hoped to see what was going on there. Officials in South Africa would not let him come. They did not want a black man to visit their country. Three years later they changed their decision. Ashe was so famous, they wanted him to play in the South African Open Tournament.

Ashe agreed to play. But he said he would not play if the audience was segregated. South Africa agreed to allow black spectators to attend the match. Ashe was the first black athlete to play tennis in South Africa. He went to South Africa to show people there that blacks could be free. He was to return there many times bringing this message.

In 1975, Ashe won the famous Wimbledon tennis tournament. He was the first black player to win there. Ashe was again the number one tennis player in the world.

In 1976, Ashe met Jeanne Moutoussomy. They were married in 1977. In 1987, they had a daughter, Camera.

In July 1979, Ashe was teaching tennis to some poor children in New York City. He had a heart attack. Later that year, he had heart **surgery.** The doctors said he would have to give up tennis. He was only 36.

Ashe had made his place in history. He had won 51 titles. But he didn't want to stop with this record. He wanted to use his fame to help others. As *Sports Illustrated* said, "His place in history gave him a **platform.** A platform he could either sleep on or speak from for the rest of his days. He made his choice." It was what Ashe did after his playing days were over that made him great.

Ashe did volunteer work for the American Heart Association. He helped to teach people about heart disease. He raised money for research.

Ashe was named captain of the U.S. Davis Cup team. (Ashe did not play. He managed the team.) The team won the cup in 1981 and 1982.

Ashe wrote some books. *Advantage Ashe* (1967) and *Arthur Ashe: Portrait in Motion* (1976) were both **autobiographies.** *Mastering Your Tennis Strokes* (1976) and *Ashe's Tennis Clinic* (1981) talked about how to play tennis. *Off the Court* (1981) was his third autobiography.

In 1983, Ashe had another heart operation. He went right back to work after it. In 1985, he was voted into the Tennis Hall of Fame. He was also awarded **honorary** degrees from several colleges.

Ashe realized that the story of black athletes in American sports had not been told. Using $300,000 of his own money, he began to gather information for a new book. In 1988, Ashe finished *A Hard Road to Glory.* This three-book set took him five years to write. The books were made into a TV program. Ashe won an Emmy for this work.

In 1988, Ashe learned he had **AIDS.** After his 1983 heart surgery, he had been given blood. The blood carried the deadly virus that causes AIDS. There was no cure for AIDS.

Ashe did not tell anyone he had AIDS. But someone found out. In 1992, *USA Today* was ready to print a story about it. Ashe was forced to announce that he had AIDS. Right after this, he founded the Arthur Ashe Foundation for the Defeat of AIDS (AAFDA).

Ashe did not know how much longer he had to live. But he wanted to fight AIDS around the world. There are many cases of AIDS in Africa. He decided that some of the money he raised would go there. Some of the money would go to help people with AIDS. Some would go for research.

Ashe hoped to raise $5 million. He asked the U.S. government to spend more money on AIDS research too. He gave talks around the country. In 1993, in *Days of Grace*, he said, "Talking about AIDS has become . . . the most important (job) of my life."

Ashe visited a hospital ward for children with AIDS. He told the children that he too had AIDS. He hoped that one day the disease could be stamped out. Ashe spoke many times about the need for research to help children with AIDS. Ashe funded a program at St. Jude's Hospital in Memphis for research on children with AIDS.

In 1992, *Sports Illustrated* named Arthur Ashe its "Sportsman of the Year." Ashe said it was clear that it was not because of what he had done on the courts. It was for what he had done away from the courts.

On December 1, 1992, Ashe gave what he called the most important speech of his life. He addressed the United Nations. It was World AIDS Day. In his speech, he stressed the deadliness of AIDS. He was saddened by the weak efforts against it. He said that we can wait no longer to fight AIDS around the world.

On February 7, 1993, Arthur Ashe died. Tennis players, civil rights workers, and AIDS workers **mourned** him. Heads of nations around the world mourned him. More than 6,000 people came to his funeral.

In 1997, Arthur Ashe Stadium was opened in Flushing, New York at the National Tennis Center. The stadium would be the home of the U.S. Open. The president of the USTA said, "Arthur Ashe was an outstanding tennis player. But we are naming our new stadium in his honor because Arthur Ashe was the finest human being the sport of tennis has ever known."

And in Richmond, Virginia, a statue of Ashe was unveiled on a main street in 1996. He is shown with a tennis racket in one hand and books in the other. It was as if his hometown had welcomed Arthur Ashe home at last.

Remembering the Facts

1. Where did Ashe grow up?

2. Who was Ashe's first tennis teacher?

3. Why did Ashe have to travel outside the South to enter tournaments?

4. Where did Ashe go to college?

5. What two titles did Ashe win in 1968?

6. Why did Ashe agree to play in South Africa?

7. What work did Ashe do for the American Heart Association?

8. How did Ashe get AIDS?

9. What did Ashe say was the most important job of his life?

10. What did Ashe say was the most important speech of his life?

Understanding the Story

11. How do you think Ashe used his fame to help others?

12. Why do you think *Sports Illustrated* named Ashe their 1992 "Sportsman of the Year"? (He had retired from tennis in 1979, 13 years earlier.)

Getting the Main Idea

Why do you think Arthur Ashe is a good role model for young people?

Applying What You've Learned

In June 1992, Ashe told *People* magazine: "You're not going to believe this. But having AIDS is not the greatest burden I've had in my life. Being black is." Why do you think Ashe felt this way?

Cher
Singer and Actress

A singing star for almost 40 years. A television star. An actress who has won an **Academy** Award. A film director. Cher has been all these things and more. She is truly one of a kind!

Cher was born on May 20, 1946, in El Centro, California. Her mother worked sometimes as an actress and model. By the time Cher was ten months old, her mother had left her father. She married seven more times, three of those times to Cher's father. She tried to support Cher and her sister with small singing jobs and bit parts. It was not a stable life.

Cher

Cher's mother was part **Cherokee** Indian. From her Cher got pure black hair, dark skin, and big, brown eyes.

Like her mother, Cher loved to sing. From the time she was three, she showed an unusual ability to learn the words to songs quickly. At age five, she went to see the movie *Cinderella*. On the way home, she sang every song in the movie by heart.

Cher and her family moved a lot. She went to a lot of different schools. Partly because of this, her grades began to fall.

In her book *The First Time*, Cher tells how she felt about school. "My spelling was terrible. I couldn't read quickly enough to get my homework done. Math was like trying to understand **Sanskrit**." (Sanskrit is a very old language of India.)

"It was embarrassing for me. I could not do the schoolwork that everyone else was doing. Was I stupid? I didn't think I was. But all the signs pointed in that direction. I couldn't understand the lessons. The only way I learned was by listening to my teachers in the classroom."

By high school, Cher still read poorly. She depended on her good memory to get by. But school was always difficult for her.

It was not until many years later that Cher learned the cause of her problem. Cher's daughter was having trouble in school. Cher knew her daughter was bright. But she was having learning problems just like Cher. When Cher took her daughter to get tested, she got a real surprise. Her daughter had a learning disability (**dyslexia**). And so did Cher.

Today we know dyslexia makes it hard to read and understand written words. But when Cher was growing up, no one understood dyslexia. There was no help for kids with this learning problem. Often they got tired of failing. Then they dropped out of school.

That is just what happened to Cher. She quit school at 16. She was in the 11th grade. She left home and moved to Los Angeles. There she stayed with a friend.

Cher had always wanted to be in show business. She did not think she could be a singer or an actress. Most stars were beautiful. Cher didn't think she was pretty. She didn't think she had that much talent either. She decided she just wanted to "be famous."

After she quit school, Cher decided to take acting lessons. This turned out to be the turning point of her life. In acting class, she finally found something she was good at. She learned that through acting, she could "make people feel." Cher had found her life's work.

Cher was 16 when she met Sonny Bono. Sonny was 28 and worked for a record producer. He got Cher jobs singing backup for different singing groups. Cher was too nervous to sing by herself. So Sonny, who could barely carry a tune, sang with her. Surprisingly, they sounded good together.

Sonny and Cher began writing songs. They started singing in small clubs. They also sang in bowling alleys and skating rinks. They called themselves "Sonny and Cher." In 1964, they got married.

In 1965, Sonny wrote "I Got You, Babe." This song sold three million copies. As Cher put it, "We got famous in about a minute and a half. Everything was fresh and strange and exciting. There was no way we could be ready for it."

For the next few years, Sonny and Cher were at the top of the folk rock craze. They turned out hit after hit. "The Beat Goes On" and "Bang, Bang" were two of these. They also starred in a movie called *Good Times.*

But this part of their life was to end soon. By 1968, their act had seen better days. Newer forms of rock and roll had passed them by. Their young fans now loved the Beatles, Jimi Hendrix, and Cream.

So Sonny and Cher changed their act. They wore evening wear and sang in nightclubs. They sang in Las Vegas. In 1969, their daughter Chastity was born.

In 1971, CBS asked them to do a television show. It was called *The Sonny and Cher Show.* The show was a big hit. People loved their singing. Everyone loved the way they joked and teased each other. They ended each show with the song "I Got You, Babe."

Cher was now known as the most beautiful woman on television. She had a string of hit records. Two of these were "Gypsies, Tramps and Thieves" and "Half Breed." She was now famous around the world.

But things were not going well at home. In 1974, Sonny and Cher **divorced.** They came back together to do *The Sonny and Cher Show* in 1976–77.

The next year, Cher married Gregg Allman. He was a rock star who had an alcohol and drug problem. The marriage did not last. Cher filed for divorce after just nine days. But a son was born to the couple. Cher named him Elijah Blue.

In the late 1970s, Cher took her solo act to Las Vegas. She earned $300,000 a week singing and cracking jokes. She was famous. But she was not happy. She felt that she had won fame without ever doing anything meaningful. Cher decided to go into acting.

She met with filmmakers. But she got no offers. She was Cher, the singing star. No one could see past her old act. It was a very **trying** time for Cher.

Finally, she landed a small part in a Broadway play. The play bombed. But Cher got great reviews. Critics agreed that she had the ability to become a major movie talent.

Soon she was offered a part in the movie *Silkwood*. Some people laughed at the idea of Cher playing with Meryl Streep. But everyone was stunned when the movie came out. Cher was called an acting marvel. *Silkwood* was one of 1984's best films. Cher was **nominated** for an Academy Award.

The next year Cher starred in the movie *Mask*. She played the mother of a teenaged boy named Rocky who died young. Rocky had a disease that made his head very large and out-of-shape. For this role, Cher won an award for best actress at the 1985 Cannes Film Festival. Later, Cher said that children like Rocky have taught her what beauty really is.

1986 and 1987 were good years for Cher. She was in great demand. She had a hit **album.** She worked on three major movies that came out in 1987. These were *Moonstruck, The Witches of Eastwick,* and *Suspect.*

In 1988, Cher landed on top! She won an Academy Award for Best Actress for the movie *Moonstruck.* Then in 1989 she won the People's Choice Award for favorite female entertainer.

In 1990, Cher had another hit album, *Heart of Stone.* She toured the country to promote the album.

Cher also became an author. In 1990, she wrote a book on diet and fitness called *Forever Fit.* In 1991, Cher did her first exercise video. It was followed by a second in 1992.

In 1996, Cher directed her first film. It was one part of HBO's three-part film *If These Walls Could Talk.*

In 1998, she wrote her **autobiography.** It was called *The First Time.* In it she tells the story of her life in an honest and funny way.

Cher works for many good causes. She supports dyslexia groups. She works to save the **environment.** She supports causes that help the homeless. But her favorite cause is the Children's **Craniofacial** Association. This group helps children with the disease that Rocky had.

In January 1998, Sonny Bono died in a skiing accident. Cher was shocked. Even though they had divorced 24 years before, she was sad at his death. She said that his death was "something she never planned to get over."

In the fall of 1998, Cher went on tour with her new album, *Believe.* It became the best-selling album of her 35 years in recording. By 1999 the title song was number one on the American Top 40. Cher became the oldest woman ever to hit the top spot. In 2000, Cher won her first Grammy Award for "Believe."

In "Believe," Cher sings:

"Well I know that I'll get through this

'Cos I know that I am strong . . ."

She certainly is! Cher has been a star of American music and show business for years. Her failures have only made her try harder. She has been a success in the movies, on television, and in music. She will probably find many new challenges ahead!

Remembering the Facts

1. What talent did Cher show at an early age?

2. What American Indian group is Cher's mother from?

3. Why did Cher have trouble learning to read?

4. How did Cher learn things in school?

5. Why did Cher drop out of school?

6. How did the acting lessons Cher took at 16 help her?

7. What song made Sonny and Cher famous?

8. What award did Cher win for the movie *Moonstruck?*

9. What award did Cher win for the song "Believe"?

10. Name a good cause Cher works for.

Understanding the Story

11. Why do you think Cher always got in trouble in school?

12. Why do you think Cher's fame has been long-lasting?

Getting the Main Idea

In what way do you think Cher is a good role model for young people?

Applying What You've Learned

Imagine that you are unable to read well. What do you think would be some ways to handle this problem?

Connie Briscoe
Author

Connie Briscoe is an African-American writer. Her best-selling **novels** tell about the lives of black women. She writes about racism and slavery. She writes about women's issues.

Connie was born on December 31, 1952, in Washington, D.C. A sister was born two years later.

Connie was born with a **moderate** hearing loss. She went to public schools. She didn't use a **hearing aid.** But for years she had lessons in **lip-reading.** She learned to speak clearly. Connie was a happy child, but shy.

Connie got her high school **diploma.** She went on to Hampton University in Virginia. She got her college degree.

Connie did not need an **interpreter** in college. It was a small school, and the classrooms were small. She depended on lip-reading and the hearing she had left.

When Connie turned 20, her hearing began to get worse. She needed to wear a hearing aid. But it wasn't long until that didn't help either. Connie had lost her hearing. By the age of 30, she was totally deaf.

It was a hard time for Connie. She told the *New York Times,* "First, you can't hear things on the phone. Then you can't hear it ring. You make excuses for what's happening. Then you get to the point you can't ignore it anymore." Connie visited doctor after doctor, hoping for a cure. When she knew there was no hope, it took some time for her to adjust. Her family stood by her in this difficult time.

Briscoe got a job at a **computer** firm. Then she got a job as an **editor** at the Joint Center for Political Studies in Washington, D.C. But there were problems. Since she could not use the telephone, she couldn't do her job well. She was passed over for **promotions.**

Briscoe learned about Gallaudet University. It is the only university for the deaf in the United States. She became an editor for the *American Annals of the Deaf.* Gallaudet **publishes** this magazine. Briscoe worked her way up to the job of managing editor of the magazine. She also learned to use and understand sign language.

Being an editor was a good job. But Briscoe found that it wasn't what she wanted to do for the rest of her life. She realized that she wanted to write books.

She remembered that she had dreamed about writing when she was a young girl. But back in the 1960s, she did not think this was something that a black woman could do. As she grew older she changed her mind. She told *Essence* in 1999, "The need to work with the written word was so strong. I believe I was preparing myself slowly. . . . I can see how I was inching toward that novel. Working as an editor was part of that process. I became a better writer."

In the summer of 1991, Briscoe got the idea of writing a novel about middle-class black women. By December she had finished three chapters. She went to the library and looked up a list of agents. An agent is a person who works with publishers. Agents try to help writers sell their books to publishers. Briscoe hired an agent. The agent gave the chapters to five publishers. One of them wanted to publish the book.

The book, *Sisters and Lovers,* was published in 1994. Briscoe was proud. She told *Essence* in 1994, "I wrote a book with 500 pages and got a major publishing company to publish it. I am proud I can be an example for other African-American writers. It shows they can do it too!"

Sisters and Lovers was the story of three sisters and the men they loved. The frank and funny tale told of the everyday lives of the sisters. Briscoe was amazed when it sold more than 100,000 copies in **hardcover** and half a million in **paperback.** The book was on lists of best-sellers all over the country. Briscoe made a lot of money from sales of her book. She quit her job. Now she could write full time.

Critics loved *Sisters and Lovers.* They found it both touching and funny. All agreed that Briscoe was a "truly fresh new voice."

Briscoe's next book was *Big Girls Don't Cry.* It was published in 1996. In it she wrote about the difficulties women and **minorities** have being accepted in high-tech jobs. It tells the story of one woman's search for love and meaning in a world where it seems hard to have both. This book made the *New York Times* best-seller list.

Briscoe wrote a different kind of book next. *A Long Way from Home* was published in 1999. It is the story of slave women struggling to survive against the odds. It is a story of slavery, freedom, and the bonds of love and family.

A Long Way from Home tells the story of three generations of slave women. All were born and trained as house slaves on the **plantation** of President James Madison and his wife Dolley. The story begins with Susie. She is the personal maid of Dolley Madison. When Susie's child Clara is born, both are treated well.

Susie knows of no life beyond the plantation. But Clara wants more. Susie tells her, "You don't know a thing about freedom, 'cause I don't know anything about it. It takes money and know-how to live free. You don't just up and do it."

When the Madisons die, their son Todd takes over. He does not run the plantation well. Clara, who is now grown, has two daughters, Ellen and Susan. The youngest girl Susan is sold to a Richmond businessman when she is 12. Her job is to take care of the man's children. After the Civil War, Susan is freed. Susan is Connie Briscoe's great-great-grandmother.

To write this book, Briscoe studied her own family history. She traced her family tree. She found that her great-great-grandmother was a slave on the Madison plantation. Briscoe talked to family members. She asked them to remember old stories they had heard. She learned a lot about her family.

There were a lot of gaps in the story. So she spent a lot of time in the library. She studied what life was like during that period for slaves in the big houses. She found that there is not a lot of information on the lives of female slaves. Only very recently has any **research** been done in this area.

Briscoe found that she loved doing research. She loved finding old stories, photos, or family bibles. There were surprises everywhere she looked.

She also learned that much information had been lost. All of the personal records of the Madisons had been destroyed. More information was lost during the Civil War. There were a lot of things she could not find. So, some of the things in the book came from her imagination. Sometimes she had to guess what some parts of life were like for the slave women.

Briscoe told *Essence* that as she did her research she found "the usual tales of whippings and (sadness). But she also found stories of love and hope." Although slavery was bleak, the people made some good times happen.

Briscoe said that the past wrongs suffered by blacks could make them strong today. She said in *Essence* that it is important for black people to know their history. She says, "In order to move forward, we must understand the past."

She hopes that her book will inspire other blacks to look at their past. She told *Black Issues* that black people need to "get out there and talk to older family members while we still can. The stories that have been handed down are a rich [gift]."

In the July 1999 issue of *Essence* she wrote: "The [slaves] used their wits and their [brains] to carve out a [life they could bear]. If they could do so much back then, I have no excuse on Earth for not getting ahead now. This is the message we ought to be handing down to our children."

To promote her books, Briscoe goes on book tours. When she does **interviews** for radio or television, Briscoe must use an interpreter. She wants to be sure she understands the questions correctly.

Often bookstores hold events in which she signs copies of her books for people. At those, she usually needs an interpreter. She wants to be sure she understands how the people want their book signed.

Briscoe uses a special telephone called a TTY. She can use it to talk to hearing or deaf people. A hearing person tells their question to the TTY operator. The operator types the question. Briscoe can read the question on her special phone. She can then type her answer back to the operator who reads it aloud. If two deaf people want to talk, they type directly back and forth to each other. It is not fast. But it works very well.

Briscoe gives talks to young people. She advises young deaf writers to learn the English language well. She says that the only way to master the language is to practice writing.

Briscoe is often asked if she plans to write about a deaf character. It is something she is thinking about. She knows how she feels about being black and female. But she has not had time to think through how being deaf has affected her. She says that she is not quite ready to write that book.

Connie Briscoe has followed the dream of her childhood. For years she did not think it was possible for her to be a writer. When she lost her hearing, that dream seemed even more impossible. But she didn't let it hold her back. She adapted to being deaf and went on. Today she is the most successful black deaf writer in the United States!

Remembering the Facts

1. Where was Connie Briscoe born and raised?

2. Why didn't she need an interpreter or hearing aid in school?

3. How old was Briscoe when she lost all of her hearing?

4. For what magazine was Briscoe managing editor?

5. Why didn't Briscoe become a writer when she was younger?

6. What was the name of Briscoe's first novel?

7. What is the name of Briscoe's novel about slavery?

8. Name three places Briscoe got information for this book.

9. Why does Briscoe often use an interpreter for interviews?

10. What is the name of the special telephone used by the deaf?

Understanding the Story

11. Why do you think Briscoe told young writers, "The only way to master the language is to practice writing?"

12. What do you think Briscoe means when she said, "If they could do so much back then, I have no excuse on Earth for not getting ahead now"?

Getting the Main Idea

Why do you think Connie Briscoe is a good role model for young people today?

Applying What You've Learned

Imagine that you woke up tomorrow and found that you were deaf. In what ways would your daily life change?

Ann Bancroft
Explorer

It is summer in **Antarctica.** Even so, it may be –70 °F. Winds may blow at 100 miles an hour. When this happens, you can see nothing but a blinding wall of white all around you.

In the summer, it is light 24 hours a day. But there is not much to see. The land is bare. There are no trees. No animals. No people. Nothing but ice and snow.

Ann Bancroft

It is the coldest place on earth. It is the windiest place on earth. And it is drier than a desert. Antarctica is not a popular spot to visit!

But this is the land that Ann Bancroft loves. She was the first woman to travel to the North Pole. She was the first woman to travel to the South Pole. And she was the first to ski all the way across Antarctica!

Ann Bancroft was born in Mendota Heights, Minnesota, in 1955. She was the second of five children. Her father sold insurance. Her mother stayed home to take care of the children. The family lived in an old farmhouse. Ann and her siblings explored the outdoors.

When Ann was 10, the family went to Kenya, East Africa. Her parents worked there as **missionaries.** (They did the work of a church.) Ann loved this time. When it was time to go back to the United States, Ann didn't want to leave.

When Ann returned, she entered seventh grade. She had always struggled in school. She was a very poor reader. And it was hard for her to remember what she read. Now she found she couldn't keep up with the other kids. Finally, she found out that she had **dyslexia.**

Dyslexia is a kind of **learning disability.** Dyslexic people have trouble with reading. They may reverse numbers and letters. For example, they may confuse the letters "b" and "d." They often mix up the directions "right" and "left."

Ann spent long hours at night studying. She went over and over her work. Finally, she was able to finish high school.

The only thing Ann had enjoyed during her school years was sports. She also loved the camps she went to during vacations. When she was old enough, she became a camp counselor. She taught others about canoeing and camping. Ann liked to teach. She began thinking about going to college to get the skills she would need to be a teacher.

Ann entered the teacher education program at the University of Oregon. She struggled with the work. Ann passed her classes. But to do student teaching, students had to have a B average. Ann's grades were not that good.

To improve her grades, Ann took some classes over. Still her grades were low. Ann's professor told her to give up on being a teacher. Ann refused. Teaching was her dream. Ann had to go before a special committee and give the reasons why she wanted to be a teacher. Finally, they agreed to let her do her student teaching.

Ann knew that once she was in the classroom, she would do fine. Sure enough, she was a natural teacher. She passed the student teaching course. And she got her college degree.

In June 1983, Ann and a friend named Tim climbed Mt. McKinley in Alaska. At 20,320 feet tall, it is the highest peak in North America. The climb took 17 days. On the way back, the climbers were tired. But something else was wrong. Tim had **hypothermia.** He was so cold his body temperature was dropping. He was becoming confused and losing control of himself. Ann got Tim down the mountain to the tent safely.

Two years later, in 1985, Ann was asked to join a team that would go to the North Pole. It would be the first trip to the North Pole by dogsled and skis. They would carry all their own equipment. National Geographic agreed to **sponsor** the team led by Will Steger. Ann was the only woman on the team.

The team trained for more than a year. But nothing could prepare them for what lay ahead. There was no way they could really understand how cold, tired, and hungry they would be. There was no way to know that they would have to fight their way for hours to gain just a few yards.

On March 7, 1986, the group set out. They had 49 sled dogs. There were five sleds to carry three tons of food and supplies. The first day they fought the ice for hours. When night came, they found they had made only one and a half miles.

Ann's worst moment on the trip came when an ice shelf she was standing on broke off. She fell into the cold Arctic Ocean. She pulled herself out. Had she stayed in the water, she would have died in minutes. Ann stayed calm. She said, "It was a good day for a dunk." She meant that it was "warm" that day: –30 °F. It was days before she felt warm again! But she never complained.

On May 3, 1986, the group reached the pole. It had taken 55 days to travel the 1,000 miles. It was a great victory! And Ann Bancroft was the first woman to reach the North Pole over the ice!

Surprisingly, Ann had not had enough of ice and snow. In 1989, she began planning a trip to ski to the South Pole. The team would be made up of four women. Getting the money for the trip was a problem. Usually companies sponsor such **expeditions.** But no one wanted to give Ann money. They thought that a team made of women would not succeed. Ann raised money from friends and family instead. And the women used their own money.

While money was being raised, Ann trained several hours a day. She ran. She lifted weights. She rode a bicycle, and she skied. In 1992, as a training exercise, Ann led her team across Greenland on skis. They were the first American women to make that trip.

One of the goals of the trip was to teach schoolchildren about Antarctica. Ann wrote lesson plans to be used by teachers. Also a web site was set up so children could follow the trip on the Internet. Over 200,000 kids did just that.

The women also hoped to send a strong message to girls. They wanted to show that women could be strong. They wanted to change people's ideas about what women can and can't do. Ann said, "I hope we can give girls and women the courage and strength to make a difference."

They also wanted the expedition to have little effect on the **environment.** They would leave no trash behind. They would carry out whatever they carried in. They would use no dogs or motor vehicles.

On November 9, 1992, the four women arrived in Antarctica. They chose this time of year because it is summer then. Even so, they faced wind chills of –70 °F. The sun shone 24 hours a day.

The team knew they had what it took to reach their goal. But many other people were not so sure. The day they were dropped at the starting point by plane, the pilot joked with them. He said that he would be back in three days to pick them up. He didn't think the women would be tough enough to stand the challenge.

The team followed the same pattern every day. They skied eight to ten hours a day. Rarely could they go over one mile an hour. Each woman was pulling a sled loaded with 200 pounds of food and supplies. They would ski for two hours. Then they took a short break to rest and eat.

All this exercise meant the women needed lots of food. Ann said the group became "human furnaces." To give them energy and keep them warm, the women needed a lot of calories, about 7,000 per day. They had to eat many foods that were high in fat. The food also had to be easy to fix and easy to carry. They ate oatmeal with butter and peanut butter. They ate **pemmican** (a mixture of dried beef and fat). They also ate a lot of cheese. Raisins, candy, cocoa, chocolate, and nuts were also on the list.

Of course, everyone dressed warmly. They wore many layers of clothes. Each woman wore a "polar suit." These were windproof and waterproof but still could "breathe." This is important because if moisture is trapped inside the clothes, the person will get damp and cold. They wore face masks all the time to keep their faces from getting frostbite. Long underwear, warm socks, ski gloves, and special boots made out of **sealskin** and **moose hide** finished the look!

The hardest time to keep warm was at night. The women had sleeping bags that were 14 inches thick. But that wasn't enough. They had to sleep in all their clothes and keep their face masks on. In fact, none of the women changed clothes or took a shower during the whole trip!

The last weeks of the trek were the hardest. One woman sprained her ankle. Another got a bad cough. Everyone had some **frostbite.** And worst of all, as they got nearer to the South Pole, the land began sloping uphill! By the time they arrived at the South Pole, they had climbed to 10,000 feet. This was not easy to do on skis!

On January 14, 1993, the group reached the South Pole. They had skied 660 miles. The trek had taken 67 days. Ann was thrilled to have met her goal.

Ann returned to Minnesota. But it wasn't long before she began missing "the ice." She began planning another trip to Antarctica. This time she hoped to ski all the way across Antarctica. Her partner would be Liv Arnesen. Liv was a teacher from Norway who had once skied by herself to the South Pole.

Ann knew the trip would cost about $1,500,000. She set up Base Camp Promotions to get sponsors for the trip. They sold ads on the expedition's web site to raise money.

Again, Ann wanted to use this trip to teach children. She wrote activities for teachers to use. She set up a web site. Through this site (www.yourexpedition.com), Ann and Liv wrote updates for teachers and students every day during the trip.

Finally, everything was ready. On November 14, 2000, Ann and Liv were back on the ice.

On February 12, 2001, the pair reached their goal. They had crossed Antarctica! It had taken 90 days to ski the 1,688 miles across the landmass of Antarctica.

In 1999, Ann Bancroft was featured in the book *Women of Courage.* In the book, she said, "Often [the things] we're known for are not the things that required the greatest courage. I became . . . known as the first woman to cross the ice to the North Pole. Later, [I put] together my own all-women trip to the South Pole.

"Yet, when I look back, neither Pole was my [big] moment of courage. . . . The hardest thing I have ever done had nothing to do with [the Poles]. It had to do with . . . something I was never expected to do: finish college, get my degree, become a teacher. . . .

"As it turns out, my learning disability and my struggle to get through school was . . . training I would use later on when I needed courage [and the ability to stick to my goals].

"Ten years later, standing in the bitter cold at the North Pole, I . . . thought, 'This is not worse than school.' When I was having a bad day on the Arctic ice, that's what I would [think of] to keep me going: 'School was harder. . . .'"

Ann has had many honors. In 1995, she was voted into the National Women's Hall of Fame. In 1987, she was named *Ms.* magazine's Woman of the Year. In 1998, she was part of the book *Remarkable Women of the Twentieth Century.*

Ann has done volunteer work for groups that help those with **multiple sclerosis, cerebral palsy,** and learning disabilities. She works with the Special Olympics. She has taught at Wilderness Inquiry. This program helps people with disabilities have outdoors adventures.

An explorer. A teacher. A volunteer for good causes. Ann Bancroft is a role model for all of us. She has shown that she has the courage to work hard for success!

Remembering the Facts

1. In what state did Ann grow up?

2. Why did Ann struggle in school?

3. Why was Ann told to give up her dream of teaching?

4. What "first" did Ann achieve in 1986?

5. Why did Ann have trouble getting sponsors for her 1989 Antarctica trek?

6. What message did Ann want to send to young girls?

7. How did Ann use her trips to teach children about Antarctica?

8. Why did the women need so many calories on the trip?

9. What "first" did Ann and Liv achieve in 2001?

10. How far did Ann and Liv ski, and how long did it take?

Understanding the Story

11. Ann said that she went on the trek to the North Pole to get to know herself better. How do you think such a trip would help you do this?

12. What did Ann say was the greatest challenge of her life? Why?

Getting the Main Idea

Why do you think Ann Bancroft is a good role model for young people today?

Applying What You've Learned

Imagine that you are going on an expedition to the North or South Pole. What do you think would be the greatest challenge to you on this kind of trip? Explain your choice.

Mark Wellman
Mountain Climber

"Everyone faces the world with different abilities and **disabilities.** But everyone has at least one goal in common . . . to break through their own **barriers.**" That is the message Mark Wellman has for everyone.

Mark Wellman

In 1982, Mark had a bad fall when mountain climbing. He became a **paraplegic.** (That means he lost the use of his legs.)

Mark did not give up on life. He became a park ranger. He designed equipment to help other disabled people enjoy sports. He learned to play wheelchair tennis. And he learned to climb mountains again. He did this using only his arms! He climbed the **sheer** faces of **El Capitan** and **Half Dome.** These mountains are in Yosemite National Park. He did not stop to feel sorry for himself. He took charge. As he did so, he stunned the world!

Mark Wellman was born in 1960. He grew up in Palo Alto, California. His father owned a donut shop and later a little coffee shop. His mother was a teacher's aide. Mark had a younger sister, Elaine.

When he was six, Mark got his first taste of adventure. He and his dad went on an overnight camping trip. They hiked for miles through the wild country. Finally, they stopped for the night. It was

Mark's first time sleeping outdoors. Strange noises kept him awake most of the night. The next day, he was glad to go home to his own bed. But the trip had started something. All his life, Mark kept going back for more.

Mark was eight when he climbed his first mountain. Mt. Lassen is 10,457 feet tall. But there is a trail to follow. Mark and his Uncle John hiked to the top! Mark thought he was on top of the world.

As Mark grew older, his uncle took him on long hiking trips. For ten days at a time, they would disappear into the back country. Mark learned to fish. He became a skilled map-reader. When he learned to use a **compass,** his uncle let him set their course. Mark became a real student of the outdoors.

School was another matter. Mark couldn't keep his mind on his work. Most subjects were hard for him. He did enjoy physical education (PE) and wood shop. There he could see the results of his work.

In high school Mark started mountain climbing with his friend Peter. They started with small peaks. They tried bigger and bigger peaks. Soon they were climbing the biggest mountains in the Sierra Nevada Mountains.

After high school, Mark's friends all went off to college. But Mark had no plans. His grades were only fair. He was not interested in going to college. All he cared about was learning more about the mountains. He wanted to improve his climbing and skiing. So, he stayed home and got a job at a store called the Ski Hut.

On August 19, 1982, Mark and Peter decided to climb a peak called Seven Gables in the Sierra Nevada range. The friends got a late start. When they reached the top, it was late afternoon. It was much too late to be on top of a mountain. And they knew it.

They were tired. It was getting dark. And they had left their flashlights back in camp. But Mark wasn't worried. He moved quickly like a mountain goat from rock to rock. At 22, he had been climbing for years.

Then Mark stepped on some loose rocks. He began to fall head over heels. There was nothing to hold onto. He flew through the air and crashed onto the rocks far below. There he lay, hurting all over. He could not move.

There was no way Peter could carry him. He made Mark as comfortable as he could. He put his sweater over Mark. He put water and some M&Ms near his head. Then he started climbing down the mountain to get help. It was 20 miles to the nearest road.

Mark was in great danger. As night fell, it began to get cold. Soon it was well below freezing. To make things worse, the wind began to howl. Soon the sweater blew off. Mark was wearing only a T-shirt and shorts. He began to fear that he would not live through the night.

Morning did come, and Mark was still alive. At 3:00 the next afternoon, the rescue team spotted him. A few hours later, Mark arrived at Valley Medical Center in Fresno. When Peter walked into his room, Mark said, "Peter, at least we climbed the peak." Already he was showing the courage that would bring him through what he would face next. Mark would never walk again.

Mark was in the hospital for three months. Then he moved to a **rehab** center. For the next two months he worked hard to build up his strength. He learned to dress himself sitting in the wheelchair.

When Mark was able to go home, he faced another question. What would he do with his life? He felt as if he had nothing left. He could no longer climb mountains. He could no longer ski or hike. It seemed that all that he loved was gone.

Not far from Mark's home was De Anza Community College. It had one of the top PE programs for the disabled in the country. In January 1983, Mark signed up for some classes. He still didn't know what he wanted to do. But he did know the PE program at De Anza could help him get stronger. He began spending a lot of time each day working out. In a few months he had built back his upper body strength.

De Anza had a wheelchair tennis team. Mark had been a good tennis player in high school. But when he tried it from a wheelchair, he found that he needed to learn a whole new game. A year later, he was playing in **tournaments.** He traveled up and down the West Coast playing tennis. At the national wheelchair tournament in 1985, he won sixth place in his division.

Mark was 24 years old. He felt that it was time for him to get a real job. He decided he wanted to be a park ranger. A nearby college offered a park management program. Mark signed up. He found that he liked all the subjects in the program. He stayed up late studying. He paid attention in class. He found that he was a good student when the subject interested him.

Mark got his first job as a park ranger at Yosemite National Park. His first job was to sit in the entrance booth and collect the $3 fee. It was a start. And the best part came on his days off. Mark wheeled himself along the miles of flat paths in the park. It was beautiful. Mark was happy to be in the country he loved.

Later Mark was asked to collect camping fees. He had to drive the ranger truck. He bolted hand controls onto the steering column. These let him use his hands to work the gas and brake pedals.

The next year Mark worked at the visitors' center. He answered people's questions about the park. At night he gave fireside talks and slide shows.

Mark wanted to make Yosemite easier for disabled people to visit. He was made director of the **handicapped access** program. He told park leaders where wheelchair ramps were needed. He pointed out places to put curb cuts. And he gave advice about a new trail to be made for those in wheelchairs.

During the winters, Mark returned to skiing. He used a sit-ski. This looked a little like a tub on a ski. It was more like sledding than skiing. But it was fun.

Mark thought other disabled people would enjoy skiing. In 1988–89 he worked to develop a program for disabled skiers at Badger Pass. There were sit-skis for paraplegics. There were special poles for people missing a leg or arm. And there were bibs and leashes for blind skiers. These allowed a sighted person to lead a blind person down the slope. This program for disabled skiers is still in place today. Many disabled people have enjoyed skiing thanks to Mark's work.

Next Mark learned to use a **kayak.** Once he was in the water, he could travel as well as anyone. It gave him a real feeling of freedom.

After a few years, Mark began thinking about climbing again. The peak he wanted to climb was El Capitan. It is the highest sheer rock wall in the United States. All Mark needed was a good climbing partner. When he met Mike Corbett, he knew he had found the man. Mike had climbed El Capitan 41 times, more than anyone else. And he was excited about climbing with Mark.

It would be a climb unlike any ever made before. No paraplegic had ever climbed a mountain. They would have to design their own equipment. They would have to decide how it could be done. They would have to think through all the problems they might face.

This is what they did. Mike climbed up first. He put a rope in place for Mark to climb. Mark clipped a pull-up bar and a rig called a **Gibbs ascender** onto the rope. He slid the bar upwards. Then he did a pull-up on it. When the Gibbs ascender on his waist was clicked into place, it took his weight. He then slid the bar up and did another pull-up. Each pull-up raised his body about six inches. El Capitan is 3,600 feet high. That is a lot of pull-ups!

They set the date of the climb for July 19, 1989. Soon people all over the country knew about the planned climb. National TV covered their climb. It was the top story on the news every night for the eight days of the climb. It was hard work. But Mark made it the whole way. He was the first paraplegic to climb a mountain!

After the climb, President Bush invited Mark and Mike to the White House. At the meeting they presented Bush with the American flag they had carried to the top. For the next year, Mark was busy. He got many awards. He signed autographs. He appeared on TV shows.

But all he really wanted was to climb again. The two men made a plan to climb Yosemite's other big wall, Half Dome. This time they decided to make the climb a fundraiser. They wanted to earn money for the Boy Scouts' program for disabled boys. They also wanted to help the park's handicapped access program.

The climb of Half Dome began on September 4, 1991. It took them 13 days to reach the top of the 2,200-foot wall. Mark's fame grew. Companies wanted him to appear in their ads. Outdoor companies offered him money to support his adventures. Mark decided to quit his job as a park ranger. He would become a full-time adventurer.

In April 1992, Mark competed as a member of the U.S. Disabled Ski Team. He used a new kind of ski called a mono-ski. The mono-ski had a special seat. Between the ski and the seat was a shock absorber. It would move up and down like a person's knees. Mark could control the ski using hand controls. Mark didn't win a medal. But it was an exciting time.

In the spring of 1993, Mark reached another goal. He skied across the Sierra Nevada mountain range using only his arms. The 50-mile trip took four days.

Mark told his story in his **autobiography,** *Climbing Back.* He has produced two videos. In *No Barriers* he tells the story of his famous climbs. In *Beyond the Barriers* many disabled adventurers are shown.

Mark Wellman now lives in Truckee, California. He owns his own business, called No Limits. He sells equipment that he has designed for disabled athletes. He tours the country speaking about disabilities.

Mark Wellman's message is for everyone. He says that his disability is easy to see. But everyone has some kind of disability that can hold him or her back in life. Maybe you are shy. Maybe you can't read well. Maybe you worry about how you look. It doesn't matter what the handicap is. You have to realize that no one can climb your mountains for you. You will have to overcome your problems for yourself.

Mark ends *Climbing Back* with words from the writer Goethe. "Whatever you can do, or dream you can, begin it. Boldness has genius, power, and magic in it."

Remembering the Facts

1. What was the first mountain Mark Wellman climbed?

2. Why didn't Mark like school?

3. What was the last mountain Mark climbed using his legs?

4. Where did Mark work as a park ranger?

5. What program did Mark direct at Yosemite?

6. How did Mark climb El Capitan?

7. Who was his climbing partner?

8. What climb did Mark make in 1991?

9. What kind of ski did Mark use on the ski team?

10. What is the name of Mark's autobiography?

Understanding the Story

11. Bob Dole once said, "*Disabled* does not mean *unable.*" How do you think Mark Wellman has shown this to be true?

12. What do you think would be the hardest daily task for you if you were a paraplegic?

Getting the Main Idea

How do you think Mark Wellman is a role model for all Americans, whether or not they are disabled?

Applying What You've Learned

Imagine a simple daily task. It could be cooking, dressing, etc. How would you do this task if you were in a wheelchair?

Chris Burke
Actor

When Chris Burke was born, the doctor gave his parents some advice. "He'll never walk or talk. He won't amount to anything. Put him in an **institution.** Forget you ever had him. It will be the best thing for you and for your family."

Chris had been born with **Down syndrome.** That is why the doctor told Chris's parents to send him away.

But the Burkes did not listen to the doctor. They took Chris home. They raised him as they did their other three children.

No one would have guessed what life had in store for Chris. He became a TV star. He made his first

Chris Burke

million dollars before he turned 30. Chris uses his fame to help others who have Down syndrome.

Chris Burke was born on August 26, 1965, in New York City. His father was a policeman. His mother stayed at home to care for their children. Chris was the youngest of four children. The others were 12, 14, and 16 when he was born.

The nurses in the hospital saw that Chris was different. His face was round and flat. His eyes were slanted. When blood tests were done, the results were clear. Chris had Down syndrome.

People with Down syndrome are not all alike. Almost all have some form of **mental retardation.** But most can learn basic skills and hold jobs. Some can live on their own with a little help.

Those with Down syndrome have poor **coordination.** Many of them have heart problems. They often have hearing problems. They sometimes have eye problems. There are a lot of other possible problems. Some of these can be corrected with surgery.

At the time Chris was born, people were **embarrassed** if they had a child with mental retardation. The children were sometimes hidden from the world. Often they were sent away to institutions.

In 1958, scientists found that people with Down syndrome had 47 instead of 46 **chromosomes.** (Chromosomes carry **genes** that determine a person's **heredity.**) When people understood what caused the **syndrome,** there was less shame about it. Still, when Chris was born in 1965, there was no help for the Burkes.

They had so many questions. What would he be able to do? Should they send him away? Were they being unfair to their other three children?

But the three older children loved Chris. They played with him and helped take care of him. They treated Chris like any other baby.

Chris went through the stages all babies do. He just went through them a little later. He talked at 18 months. He walked at two years. The older children read to Chris and played with him all the time. Chris was a happy child.

In the 1960s there were few programs to help children with Down syndrome. Even New York City had little to offer. The Burkes worked hard to find help for Chris.

They knew he would need **speech therapy.** Children with Down syndrome often have trouble speaking correctly. Their mouths are small. They have poor control of their tongue muscles. They don't understand the meaning of some words.

Today most Down syndrome children start speech therapy at a young age. But back in the 1960s, no one wanted to bother with them. Mrs. Burke finally found a therapist willing to work with Chris when he was three.

At home, Chris liked to watch a new TV show called *Sesame Street.* He loved to sing along with the songs. He set up his blocks in front of the TV. He made words from the letters they showed.

At night, he would put on shows for his family. Sometimes he would imitate the characters on the show. Chris's sister Ellen said Chris "loved to perform for us from the time he was very little. He was very musical. He had that talent early on. Before he could [speak], he was entertaining us."

When Chris was four, he started going to a play group. It was at the Kennedy Child Study Center. The center was one of the first of its kind in the United States. It offered many services for children with special needs. Chris went to play group twice a week. While he played, his mother got information from the experts at the center.

When Chris turned five, he began going to the center every day. He got along with everyone, child or adult. He loved school. Soon he could spell his name.

But what he loved best was dress-up time. Chris liked to play different parts. He still remembers his first time on stage. The children put on *The Emperor's New Clothes.* As he remembers, "That was when I decided I wanted to be an actor, when I was five years old."

Chris would perform at the drop of a hat. He knew all the latest music. Often he would sing his favorite songs. Other times he told jokes. He might put on a skit. Or he might do a dance. His family was a great audience. They always cheered and clapped.

The Burke family told Chris he had Down syndrome. They told him that was what made him a little different sometimes. They never made a big deal of it. Chris didn't like the sound of the word "down." So, he told his dad that he had "Up" syndrome instead. That sounded a lot better to Chris!

When Chris was eight, the Burkes started looking for a school for him. The public schools of New York had special education classes. The Burkes visited these classes. The children in them did little but play all day. They knew Chris could learn much more than that. So, they enrolled him in a **boarding school** near Boston.

It was a wonderful school. Chris learned a lot during the four years he was there. By the time he was nine, he was reading and doing math on a second grade level. He took part in the Special Olympics. And he kept putting on plays. Chris would think up the costumes and props. He would make up a plot. He would add music. He would even draw the tickets and hand them out. His skits were very popular with both students and teachers.

When Chris was 13, he entered a new school. 130 students, many with Down syndrome, lived at the school. Chris's language skills improved thanks to daily speech therapy.

Chris kept talking about how he was going to be a star some day. As he grew older, it began to worry his mother. She felt that it wasn't good for him to have such goals.

By the time Chris was 19, the Burkes were really worried. All he wanted to do was watch TV. He bought a VCR with his savings. Every Sunday when the TV schedule came, he set the VCR. He recorded dozens of movies. Then he watched them over and over.

Chris thought it was fine to watch so much TV. After all, he was planning to be an actor. Watching TV was preparing for his career!

It was about this time that Chris noticed that no one on TV had Down syndrome. Then in 1985, a ten-year-old boy named Jason Kingsley had a bit part on the show *The Fall Guy.* It was the first time a person with Down syndrome had played a role on a TV series. Chris wrote to Jason's mother. He told her that he planned to be an actor, too.

On a school work-study program, Chris was given a job cleaning. He liked this work. But he made it clear to his teachers that he was really on his way to Hollywood.

Meanwhile, in Hollywood, a **director** was writing the **script** for a TV **pilot.** It was called *Desperate.* In the script there was a small part for a young man with Down syndrome. Jason was too young for the part. The director called Mrs. Kingsley to see if she knew of anyone else. She did: Chris Burke!

In a few days, Chris was on his way to Hollywood. He had to try out for the part. Chris looked good on camera. He could speak fairly well. And he had good social skills. Chris got the job. If the show did well, ABC might make it into a weekly series.

The show was to be filmed in Key West. The filming took 18 days. Chris did not have a big role. But he was in several scenes. He had lines to learn. Chris soon found out it was hard work. At night he and his dad would work on the lines. Chris would write his lines on paper. Then he repeated them over and over.

Chris tried hard to listen to the director. He was careful to do what he was told. On breaks, Chris had to go back to his room to rest. If he got too tired, he would forget his lines.

When the filming was done, Chris and his dad went back to New York. Chris went back to doing volunteer work. He helped in a class for children with mental retardation at P.S. 138. When *Desperate* came on TV, the Burkes and everyone they knew watched it. Chris had done a great job. But ABC did not pick up the show for a series. Chris's acting job was over.

But at ABC they had not forgotten Chris. "He lit up the screen," said Chad Hoffman, a vice president. "He [charmed] you. . . . There was something heartwarming about him. It made you both enjoy watching him and feel really good about being with him." ABC began working on a series that would center around Chris.

The Burkes knew nothing of this. Chris was offered a paying job at P.S. 138. He would run the elevator. In February 1988, Chris started his new job. He was the first person with Down syndrome to be hired by the New York City schools. The Burkes were thrilled. This was much better than acting. It was a steady job.

It wasn't long, however, before Hollywood called again. Chris was asked to play the part of Corky Thacher, a student with Down syndrome who attends public high school. The plot would be about his struggles in his classes. It would deal with how he learns to get along with other kids. The name of the show was *Life Goes On.*

The pilot got good ratings. ABC wanted to make it into a series. Chris and his father flew to Hollywood. This time they would stay a while. Chris was under contract to do 22 shows.

It was hard work. Sometimes he had to be on the set by 6 A.M. The days were long. Sometimes he had many lines to learn. He had to learn where to stand and where to look. Often it took many takes to get a scene just right.

The show got a lot of attention. Chris and his parents were **interviewed** by newspapers and magazines. In November 1988, he made the cover of *Life* magazine. Chris was a star!

Chris was asked to speak many places. When he spoke at the National Down Syndrome convention, he said he wanted to be a spokesperson for all people with disabilities. He wanted people with Down syndrome to get the respect they should.

Chris and *Life Goes On* had a big effect on people's ideas about people with mental retardation. President George Bush asked Chris to come to the White House. There Chris made a public service announcement. He talked about what people who have Down syndrome can do.

In 1989, Chris was **nominated** for a Golden Globe Award. He was voted best actor by the Academy of Family Films. He won the 1989 Youth in Film Award. He was chosen as one of ten outstanding young Americans by the Junior Chamber of Commerce. He became the spokesperson for the National Down Syndrome Congress and the McDonald's McJobs program.

The show was **renewed** for another 22 shows in 1990–91. It was shown around the world in many different languages.

In 1992, Chris wrote his **autobiography.** It is called *A Special Kind of Hero.* He marched in President Clinton's **inaugural** parade. A New York City public school has been named in his honor. The Christopher Burke School is a school for students with disabilities.

Chris continues to guest star on many TV shows. Most recently he can be seen as Taylor on the show *Touched by an Angel.*

Chris says that the best thing about his fame is that it helps people see what a person with a disability can do, not what they can't do. He says, "Everyone needs to know that we are people too. We have dreams and hopes. . . . We laugh and have fun, and we can be serious and do a good job. We can do lots of things if people give us the chance."

Remembering the Facts

1. Why do children with Down syndrome have trouble speaking?

2. What activity did Chris like best at school?

3. Why did Chris go to boarding school at age eight?

4. Why did Chris think it was OK for him to watch a lot of TV?

5. How did Chris learn his lines for *Desperate?*

6. Why did the Burkes want Chris to keep his elevator job instead of acting?

7. In what show did Chris play Corky Thacher?

8. What is the name of Chris's autobiography?

9. What does Chris say is the best thing about his fame?

10. What kind of school is the Christopher Burke School?

Understanding the Story

11. Why do you think that doctors used to advise parents to put children with Down syndrome away in institutions instead of keeping them at home?

12. Why do you think Chris is such a good spokesperson for people with disabilities?

Getting the Main Idea

Why do you think Chris Burke is a good role model for young Americans?

Applying What You've Learned

Imagine that you are a movie director. One of your actors has Down syndrome. What things do you think that you could do to help this person do the job?

Vocabulary

Laura Bridgman: Teacher

- scarlet fever
- vibrate
- educated
- braille
- grooves
- published
- legislators

John Wesley Powell: Explorer

- education
- amputated
- exploration
- gorge
- rapids
- whitewater
- canyon
- fossils
- sextant
- barometer
- altitude
- agency
- arid

Washington Roebling: Engineer

- suspension
- engineer
- disabled
- caisson
- disease
- spanned
- engineering
- graduated
- ferry
- foundations
- amputated
- tetanus
- oxygen
- nitrogen
- paralysis
- collapsed
- paralyzed
- telescope
- genius

Franklin D. Roosevelt: President of the United States

- Great Depression
- prep school
- athlete
- senator
- Republican
- Democrat
- assistant
- nominated
- polio
- paralyzed
- Convention
- inaugural
- Works Progress Administration
- Civilian Conservation Corps
- vaccine

Katharine Hathaway: Writer

- heroine
- determination
- autobiography
- spinal tuberculosis
- hunchback
- deformed
- classic
- disability

Walt Disney: Cartoonist

- cartoon
- theater
- cartoonist
- ambulance
- salary
- animation
- feature
- Presidential

Glenn Cunningham: Runner

- athlete
- amputated
- circulation
- scholarship
- prediction
- massage
- qualified
- Olympics
- amateur
- physical education

Roy Campanella: Catcher

- physical therapy
- paralyzed
- injuries
- major leagues
- defense
- pennant
- exhibition
- commentator
- autobiography

Bernard Bragg: Actor

- autobiography
- mime
- wings
- imitating
- lip-read
- headphones
- amplifier
- vibration
- diploma
- interview
- major
- literature
- backstage
- conductor
- narrators
- residence
- doctorate
- endowed chair

Ray Charles: Musician

- genius
- soul
- jazz
- blues
- gospel
- autobiography
- boogie-woogie
- braille
- classical
- segregation
- inspired
- gleans
- inaugural

Arthur Ashe: Tennis Player

- athletes
- racial barrier
- research
- segregated
- tournaments
- scholarship
- injustice
- surgery
- platform
- autobiographies
- honorary
- AIDS
- mourned

Cher: Singer and Actress

- Academy
- Cherokee
- Sanskrit
- dyslexia
- divorced
- trying
- nominated
- album
- autobiography
- environment
- Craniofacial

Connie Briscoe: Author

- novels
- moderate
- hearing aid
- lip-reading
- diploma
- interpreter
- computer
- editor
- promotions
- publishes
- hardcover
- paperback
- critics
- minorities
- plantation
- research
- interviews

Ann Bancroft: Explorer

- Antarctica
- missionaries
- dyslexia
- learning disability
- hypothermia
- sponsor
- expeditions
- environment
- pemmican
- sealskin
- moose hide
- frostbite
- multiple sclerosis
- cerebral palsy

Mark Wellman: Mountain Climber

- disabilities
- barriers
- paraplegic
- sheer
- El Capitan
- Half Dome
- compass
- rehab
- tournaments
- handicapped access
- kayak
- Gibbs ascender
- autobiography

Chris Burke: Actor

- institution
- Down syndrome
- mental retardation
- coordination
- embarrassed
- chromosomes
- genes
- heredity
- syndrome
- speech therapy
- boarding school
- director
- script
- pilot
- interviewed
- nominated
- renewed
- autobiography
- inaugural

Answers

LAURA BRIDGMAN: TEACHER

1. She had scarlet fever.
2. They were a busy farm family. There was much work to do. Laura had two younger brothers.
3. He was a friend to her. He spent long hours with her showing her about the world. He kept alive her curiosity and desire to learn.
4. Laura became hard to handle. She had tantrums and would not easily mind.
5. He thought that the deaf-blind could be taught. Laura was bright, so she was a good first pupil.
6. key, cup, knife, fork, spoon, book
7. Her teacher spelled into her hand so she could feel the letters.
8. It was hard for her to learn the names of things she could not touch. Putting words in the right order to make sentences was hard too.
9. Charles Dickens
10. Helen Keller was taught by the same methods by Anne Sullivan.

Answers will vary:

11. Most children learn language by hearing it. A deaf child may learn by seeing signs or seeing lips move. If a child can neither see nor hear, both these ways of learning are closed.
12. They get angry because they cannot tell anyone what they want. Also, they do not understand what is going on around them or what others want them to do.

Getting the Main Idea: Laura is a good role model because she kept her love of learning even though she had many handicaps. She helped others in the ways she could. She never quit trying to learn.

Applying What You've Learned: Answers will vary.

JOHN WESLEY POWELL: EXPLORER

1. Answers will vary: Waterfalls hundreds of feet high; big whirlpools; huge waterspouts; the river disappeared underground.
2. He had lost his right arm.

3. It was not safe. He was being beaten because his father favored ending slavery.

4. He was largely self-taught.

5. One of the boats was destroyed.

6. altitude, location, direction of river, distance traveled

7. They were killed by American Indians.

8. U.S. Geographical and Geological Survey

9. *Report on the Lands of the Arid Region of the United State*s

10. language, customs, clothing, legends, history, things they made

Answers will vary:

11. He came to see the whole world as a classroom. He learned that he could learn by observing things around him.

12. He worked for many years surveying the land around the river. He wrote his findings in a book. He worked hard to get the government to adapt his ideas. He was a tireless worker in achieving all these things.

Getting the Main Idea: Powell is a good role model because he worked hard to achieve his dreams. He did not let poverty or the loss of an arm slow him down. He stood up for his beliefs, even when most other people thought he was wrong.

Applying What You've Learned: It was a remote and inaccessible area. It was a rugged and dry area not very suitable for settlement or farming.

WASHINGTON ROEBLING: ENGINEER

1. New York City and Brooklyn

2. Chester Arthur

3. Rensselaer Polytechnic Institute

4. building bridges

5. It was inconvenient for so many people to travel back and forth by ferry.

6. John Roebling, Washington's father

7. Dirt was shoveled out. Rocks were chipped up and removed.

8. They came up too quickly from an area of high pressure to an area of lower air pressure.

9. He sent messages by his wife. He observed from his window.

10. steel

Answers will vary:

11. It was historic in several ways. It was the largest suspension bridge ever built. It was the first bridge made of steel. It joined two important American cities. It was seen as the eighth wonder of the world in its day.

12. She stood by her husband during his long years of illness. She learned about engineering so

that she could deliver messages back and forth.

Getting the Main Idea: He was a role model because he showed great courage. He continued his work even though he was paralyzed and in pain. He saw the work through to completion when many would have given up.

Applying What You've Learned: Machines have improved. The digging could be done by machines instead of men. Today we understand about the bends. There would not be illness and death due to this problem.

FRANKLIN D. ROOSEVELT: PRESIDENT OF THE UNITED STATES

1. It was a large home on 1,000 acres of land.
2. the U.S. Navy
3. the Democratic Party
4. state senator from New York
5. He learned how the Navy worked in wartime.
6. polio
7. the Great Depression
8. radio programs in which Roosevelt talked to Americans about government programs
9. World War II had begun in Europe.
10. four

Answers will vary:

11. Photographers did not want to show Roosevelt in any pose

that might have looked "weak." Roosevelt himself hid his disability as much as possible.

12. Probably not. People are more accepting of differences today.

Getting the Main Idea: He is a role model because he did not let his disability keep him from success. It would have been easy for him to retire and lead a comfortable life after his illness, but he kept going.

Applying What You've Learned: Answers will vary. The polio may have given Roosevelt compassion for those who were less fortunate. He could understand more about problems of other people.

KATHARINE HATHAWAY: WRITER

1. spinal tuberculosis
2. He was a hunchback.
3. ten years
4. They made her room the center of the house. They spent a lot of time with her.
5. She was very small and had a hunched back.
6. They tried not to look at her. They paid no attention to her.
7. Radcliffe College
8. *The Little Locksmith*
9. They were crushed into a small space.
10. 42

Answers will vary:

11. It was isolated and small. She wanted it to be full of friends and art.

12. She made a place for herself in the world.

Getting the Main Idea: She was a person of courage. She took what life gave her and found pleasure in small things. She was always positive. She kept on believing in her own worth even when others did not.

Applying What You've Learned:
A parent who works hard to provide for the family
Anyone who works to overcome a disability of any kind
A person who gives of themselves to help others

WALT DISNEY: CARTOONIST

1. Mickey Mouse

2. He painted a pig on the side of the house with a bucket of tar.

3. He couldn't pay attention. He didn't follow directions. He couldn't learn with normal methods of classroom teaching.

4. He was an ambulance driver.

5. Paper cutouts were placed on a background, then photographed. The position was changed. Then another photo was made.

6. Making many drawings of the same thing with changes in position of the moving part. Photos were made of the drawings with a movie camera.

7. "Steamboat Willie"

8. "Flowers and Trees"

9. *Snow White*

10. Disneyland

Answers will vary:

11. Disney was not a good student. He couldn't pay attention or follow directions. He did not enjoy school. Once he had seen the world during the war, he couldn't stand to go back to school.

12. He decided as a teenager what he wanted to do. He gave great effort toward achieving his goal. He was self taught. When some new technology appeared, he learned to use it. Even during the times in his life when he wasn't making money, he loved what he was doing.

Getting the Main Idea: Disney is a good role model because he never stopped working toward his goal. He worked hard to teach himself new things. He never gave up when times were hard. He stuck to his dreams even when others (like his father) did not approve.

Applying What You've Learned:
Answers will vary.

GLENN CUNNINGHAM: RUNNER

1. Atlanta, Kansas

2. In an explosion and fire, resulting from the unknowing use of gasoline to start a fire
3. Most of the toes were gone. The ball of the foot was gone.
4. three years
5. a one-mile race at the county fair
6. the University of Kansas
7. 1932, 1936
8. 4 minutes 4.4 seconds
9. to help children who were in trouble for various reasons
10. almost 10,000

Answers will vary:

11. He was so strong he was being compared to iron. He had the strength of all runners. He also had the strength to have overcome great obstacles.
12. He showed great courage. He ran in spite of pain and injury.

Getting the Main Idea: He is a good role model because he kept going when most would have given up. When he could have had fame and wealth, he gave it up to help others who needed him.

Applying What You've Learned: Answers will vary.

ROY CAMPANELLA: CATCHER

1. He had a milk route.
2. He had no equipment to protect himself.
3. the Bacharach Giants (briefly)

4. It was a professional black baseball team.
5. They didn't make enough money in the black pro league.
6. the Brooklyn Dodgers
7. 1951, 1953, and 1955
8. the Yankees
9. They retired his number.
10. coach, TV commentator

Answers will vary:

11. He did not stop living because of the accident. He made up his mind to keep going.
12. He played catcher as a boy when no one else wanted the job. He played many games with injuries as an adult. He was a hard worker.

Getting the Main Idea: Roy Campanella is a good role model because he kept his faith and courage when he was disabled. He found new ways to live a productive life. He did not give up.

Applying What You've Learned: Coaching. Working with young people. Providing money to help needy youth have opportunities to learn the sport. Writing a book. Becoming a manager.

BERNARD BRAGG: ACTOR

1. His parents and the people around him were also deaf.
2. watching his father's theater group

3. They cannot hear the sounds to imitate them. They have to learn to make sounds by looking at the position of the mouth and tongue and by feeling vibrations.

4. It is hard to learn how to put words together correctly.

5. Gallaudet College

6. the California School for the Deaf

7. Marcel Marceau

8. the National Theater of the Deaf

9. He performed on his own. He wrote and directed plays.

10. He gave money to set up an endowed chair.

Answers will vary:

11. The man turned him down because he was deaf. Maybe he thought Bragg wouldn't get along because he didn't speak well. Maybe he thought Bragg wouldn't be able to do the job. He didn't want to give him a chance. It was easier to say "no."

12. It will give a deaf artist or scholar money and time so they will be free to write about the deaf.

Getting the Main Idea: He is a role model because he worked hard to reach his goal. He did not waver from what he wanted to do.

Applying What You've Learned: It would be harder to talk to people. You couldn't hear music. It would be hard to understand what was going on in many situations.

RAY CHARLES: MUSICIAN

1. the "genius of soul"

2. Greenville, Florida

3. Mr. Pit, a neighbor

4. seven

5. St. Augustine: the Florida State School for the Deaf and the Blind

6. He does it in his head. Then he tells the notes to someone else to write down.

7. "Baby, Let Me Hold Your Hand"

8. "Georgia on My Mind"

9. the Presidential Medal of Freedom

10. soul

Answers will vary:

11. He had the talent from a very young age. He learned to play the piano at age three. He quickly soaked up styles and sounds from other musicians who were much older than he.

12. The South was segregated at that time. It would not have been usual for black musicians to play in a white club.

Getting the Main Idea: Ray Charles was born with talent. But he worked very hard to use it. He knew from a young age that he wanted to be a musician. He let nothing stand in the way of reaching his goal.

Applying What You've Learned: Probably so. He grew up listening to gospel music and the blues. He also suffered from poverty and loss at a young age. These things are a part of him and made his music what it is.

ARTHUR ASHE: TENNIS PLAYER

1. Richmond, VA
2. Ron Charity
3. He was not allowed to enter the all-white tournaments in the South.
4. UCLA
5. the Davis Cup and the U.S. Open
6. He wanted to show blacks there that blacks could be free.
7. He taught about heart disease and raised money.
8. through a blood transfusion
9. talking about AIDS
10. his speech to the United Nations about AIDS

Answers will vary:

11. He worked for the American Heart Association. He raised money to fight AIDS. He spoke about AIDS. He fought against racism and injustice in the U.S. and South Africa.
12. Ashe was still showing good sportsmanship. He was thinking about others rather than himself. He was still an outstanding sportsman, even though he no longer played tennis.

Getting the Main Idea: Ashe is a role model because he kept sports in their place in his life. He worked hard and became a champion in tennis. But when that part of his life was over, he didn't quit. He found ways to use his fame to help others.

Applying What You've Learned: Arthur Ashe spent most of his life fighting racism. He was denied many opportunities because he was black. He always had to break ground for other blacks to follow. He has a list of "firsts" to his credit. But it wasn't easy always having to break new ground. And he got tired of others putting him down and telling him he wasn't good enough. Not many black athletes played tennis at the time Arthur Ashe did. So it was always a fight for him to be accepted.

CHER: SINGER AND ACTRESS

1. singing, memorizing songs
2. Cherokee
3. She was dyslexic.
4. by listening to her teachers
5. She was discouraged with school.
6. She found something she was good at.
7. "I Got You, Babe"
8. Academy Award for Best Actress
9. Grammy Award
10. dyslexia groups, groups that help the homeless, environmental causes, the Children's Craniofacial Association

Answers will vary:

11. Often when children have trouble learning, especially reading, they act out. If they can't follow the lesson, they get bored, and try to find something to amuse themselves.

12. She is able to change when the situation changes. When one thing fails, she tries another.

Getting the Main Idea: She is a good role model because she doesn't give up when she fails, but changes directions and finds new success.

Applying What You've Learned: Answers will vary. Learning to listen better. Making lists of important things to remember. Getting tutoring to learn to read better.

CONNIE BRISCOE: AUTHOR

1. Washington, D.C.

2. She had a moderate hearing loss. She could read lips. Classes were small.

3. 30

4. *American Annals of the Deaf*

5. She didn't think it was something a black woman could do.

6. *Sisters and Lovers*

7. *A Long Way from Home*

8. (any three) her own family history, family members, library, old photos, bibles, old letters, her imagination

9. She wants to be sure she understands the questions correctly.

10. TTY

Answers will vary:

11. Writing is how a good writer trains. The more you do it, the better you are. By writing and rewriting, you learn to express yourself better.

12. The slaves had so many things to overcome. They had very few chances to better themselves. People now have many different paths open to them. It just takes desire and hard work.

Getting the Main Idea: Briscoe is a role model because she kept working to achieve her goal. Losing her hearing set her back for a while. But she didn't let it stop her.

Applying What You've Learned: You would have to read lips instead of hearing speech. You would have to read captions on TV. You couldn't hear music. If you were in school, it would be hard to follow what was happening in the classroom.

ANN BANCROFT: EXPLORER

1. Minnesota

2. She had a learning disability (dyslexia).

3. Her grades were not high enough for her to be allowed to do her student teaching.

4. She was the first woman to reach the North Pole.

5. No one believed that a group of women could achieve this goal.

6. That women could be strong. That women can do many things people don't believe they can.

7. She set up web sites on which people could track the expedition's progress. She wrote lesson plans for teachers to use.

8. It took a lot of energy for the women to keep warm and to do so much exercise.

9. They skied across the whole of Antarctica.

10. 1,688 miles. 90 days.

Answers will vary:

11. You would find out how much courage and strength you had. You would find out if you could handle being very cold, tired, and hungry. You'd see if you could work in a team.

12. The greatest challenge for her was finishing school and becoming a teacher. School was very hard for her because she had so much trouble reading.

Getting the Main Idea: She is a role model because she kept trying to reach her goals. She did not drop out of college when a teacher said she should. She finished college and got her degree. She faced great odds in putting together an all-woman trek to the South Pole. But she believed in herself and went ahead with her plan.

Applying What You've Learned: Answers will vary.

MARK WELLMAN: MOUNTAIN CLIMBER

1. Mt. Lassen

2. He couldn't keep his mind on his work, and classes were hard for him.

3. Seven Gables

4. Yosemite National Park

5. the handicapped access program

6. He used a pull-up bar and a Gibbs ascender.

7. Mike Corbett

8. Half Dome

9. a mono-ski

10. *Climbing Back*

Answers will vary:

11. People with a disability have to find a different way to achieve their goals. They may still be able to reach their goals. But they will need to be flexible and creative.

12. Answers will vary.

Getting the Main Idea: Everyone has some type of disability. It takes courage to work to overcome it. No one can do it for you. Mark realized this and worked hard to do the things he wanted to do, in spite of his disability.

Applying What You've Learned: Answers will vary.

CHRIS BURKE: ACTOR

1. Their mouths are small. Their control of their tongue muscles is poor.

2. Playing dress-up. Acting in plays.

3. The Burkes were not happy with the kind of education offered in the special ed classes in the New York public schools.

4. He was learning more about his future career.

5. He wrote them down. He said them over and over. His dad practiced with him.

6. It was a steady job with benefits. They did not think acting would work out.

7. *Life Goes On*

8. *A Special Kind of Hero*

9. He can serve as a spokesperson for other Americans with disabilities.

10. a school for children with disabilities

Answers will vary:

11. They did not think that the children would ever learn anything. They would be too much trouble to take care of. They were an embarrassment to the family. They would take time away from the other children in the home.

12. He is a good spokesperson because he himself has Down syndrome and has achieved so much.

Getting the Main Idea: Chris Burke is a role model because he kept going after what he really wanted. He understands what he can and cannot do. He has never let his limitations slow him down. He believed in himself even when everyone told him he couldn't do it.

Applying What You've Learned: Provide a good place for them to rest between scenes. Provide a tutor to help them learn their lines. Avoid too much confusion on the set.

Additional Activities

LAURA BRIDGMAN: TEACHER

1. Learn how to finger spell.
2. Read about braille.
3. Read more about the life of Laura Bridgman.
4. Read about the life of Helen Keller in *The Miracle Worker* or *Helen Keller: The Story of My Life.*
5. Find out about the Perkins School for the Blind.
6. Find out how deaf-blind children are taught today.

JOHN WESLEY POWELL: EXPLORER

1. On a map, trace Powell's route. Begin in Green River, Wyoming. End in Callville, Nevada.
2. Read about Lake Powell, which was named after John Wesley Powell.
3. It is no longer possible to take the trip down the river as Powell did. Dams block parts of the river. Read about one of these dams. They include Flaming Gorge Dam, Glen Canyon Dam, and Boulder Dam, to name a few.
4. Read more about the Grand Canyon.
5. Find out if white-water rafting is still possible on the Colorado River. Report to the class on your findings.

WASHINGTON ROEBLING: ENGINEER

1. Find out more about the bends (caisson disease).
2. Read more about the building of the Brooklyn Bridge.
3. Find out how a suspension bridge is made.
4. Talk to a diver. Learn how divers today avoid getting the bends.
5. Read about how steel is made.

FRANKLIN D. ROOSEVELT: PRESIDENT OF THE UNITED STATES

1. Find out more about polio. Learn about the Salk vaccine, which prevents this disease.

2. Read more about Roosevelt's New Deal.

3. Look up information about the FDR Memorial in Washington, D.C.

4. Eleanor Roosevelt, FDR's wife, was also an interesting person. Read more about her life.

5. Find out more about the Great Depression.

KATHARINE HATHAWAY: WRITER

1. Find out more about spinal tuberculosis.

2. Find a copy of *The Little Locksmith* or *The Journals and Letters of the Little Locksmith*. Read part of her work. Tell how it makes you feel.

WALT DISNEY: CARTOONIST

1. Watch one of the Disney classics, such as *Snow White* or *Steamboat Willie*. Report on it to the class.

2. If you have been to one of the Disney theme parks, report on it to the class.

3. If you have never visited one of the parks, look up information on the Web about one.

4. Write a paragraph telling what you would like to do if you visited that park.

5. Visit the Disney store if there is one near you. List some of the Disney products that are for sale there.

6. Write a paragraph about your favorite character in a Disney film or cartoon.

GLENN CUNNINGHAM: RUNNER

1. Read about other famous milers. Two of these are Jim Ryan and Roger Bannister.

2. Find out who won the 1,500-meter run in the last Olympics. What was their time?

3. Run a mile. Time yourself and see how close to a four-minute mile you come.

ROY CAMPANELLA: CATCHER

1. Read Roy's autobiography, *It's Good to Be Alive*.

2. Read more about the Negro National League. Find out who some of its star players were.

3. Read the story of Jackie Robinson, the first black player in the National League.

BERNARD BRAGG: ACTOR

1. Find out more about the National Theater of the Deaf.

2. Learn some signs. Use them to talk to someone who is deaf.

3. Find out what Bernard Bragg is doing now.

4. Read about Gallaudet University.

5. Learn to finger spell.

RAY CHARLES: MUSICIAN

1. Watch the videos *The Genius of Soul* (PBS) or *Fifty Years of Music Making* (Fox).

2. Watch the video *The Blues Brothers*.

3. Listen to one of Ray Charles's albums. Report on the music to the class.

4. Read Ray Charles's autobiography *Brother Ray*.

ARTHUR ASHE: TENNIS PLAYER

1. Read about Pancho Gonzales, Arthur Ashe's boyhood tennis hero.

2. Find out more about Wimbledon.

3. Find out more about the Davis Cup in tennis.

4. Look up the Arthur Ashe Foundation for the Defeat of AIDS. What work is it doing?

5. Look up the Arthur Ashe Institute for Urban Health. What work is it doing?

CHER: SINGER AND ACTRESS

1. Watch one of Cher's movies. Report on it to the class. Her best-known movies are *Silkwood, Moonstruck, Mask, The Witches of Eastwick, Mermaids,* and *Tea with Mussolini*.

2. Listen to Cher's album, *Believe.*

3. Listen to one of Sonny and Cher's recordings such as "I Got You, Babe."

4. Find out what Cher is doing now.

5. Read more about dyslexia. Find out how it affects learning.

6. Find out about the Children's Craniofacial Association, Cher's favorite cause.

CONNIE BRISCOE: AUTHOR

1. Read one of Briscoe's books.

2. Find out more about how a TTY operates. If you know someone who has one, try it out. Share your findings with the class.

3. Interview an older member of your family about your family history. Write a story about your findings.

ANN BANCROFT: EXPLORER

1. Look up the web site www.yourexpedition.com. Read the exciting story of Ann and Liv's trip across Antarctica. Watch the video. Study the maps that show where they went.

2. Read more about Antarctica.

3. Find out more about what kind of food and clothing are needed for a trip to the pole.

4. Read about other polar explorers. Some are Sir Ernest Shackleton, Robert Peary, Richard Byrd,

Robert Scott, and Matthew Hensen.

5. Read about the journey of the *Nautilus.* It was the first submarine to sail under the arctic ice cap all the way to the North Pole.

MARK WELLMAN: MOUNTAIN CLIMBER

1. Watch one of Mark's videos, *No Barriers* or *Beyond the Barriers.*

2. Read Mark's autobiography *Climbing Back.*

3. Find out more about the mountains Mark climbed, El Capitan and Half Dome.

4. Get more information on Yosemite National Park.

CHRIS BURKE: ACTOR

1. Read more about Down syndrome.

2. Find out what Chris Burke is doing today.

3. Find out about the Special Olympics.

4. Read Chris's book *A Special Kind of Hero.*

References

LAURA BRIDGMAN: TEACHER

Dickens, Charles. *American Notes.* Great Britain: Chapman & Hall, 1892.

Freeberg, Ernest. *The Education of Laura Bridgman: First Deaf and Blind Person to Learn Language.* Cambridge, MA: Harvard University Press, 2001.

Gitter, Elisabeth. *The Imprisoned Guest: Samuel Howe and Laura Bridgman, the Original Deaf-Blind Girl.* New York: Farrar Straus & Giroux, 2001.

Hunter, Edith Fisher. *Child of the Silent Night.* Boston: Houghton Mifflin Company, 1963.

JOHN WESLEY POWELL: EXPLORER

Frazee, Steve. *First Through the Grand Canyon.* Philadelphia, PA: The John C. Winston Co., 1960.

Terrell, John Upton. *The Man Who Rediscovered America.* New York: Weybright and Talley, 1969.

Worster, Donald. *A River Running West: The Life of John Wesley Powell.* New York: Oxford University Press, 2001.

WASHINGTON ROEBLING: ENGINEER

Lyttle, Richard B. *Challenged by Handicap.* Chicago: Reilly & Lee Books, 1971.

McCullough, David. *The Great Bridge: The Epic Story of the Building of the Brooklyn Bridge.* New York: Simon & Schuster, 2001.

Steinman, D.B. *The Builders of the Bridge: The Story of John Roebling and His Son.* New York: Arno Press, 1972.

FRANKLIN D. ROOSEVELT: PRESIDENT OF THE UNITED STATES

Davis, Kenneth. *FDR: Into the Storm 1937–1940: A History.* New York: Random House, 1993.

Ferrell, Robert H. *The Dying President: Franklin D. Roosevelt, 1944–45.* Columbia: University of Missouri Press, 1998.

Goodwin, Doris K. *No Ordinary Time.* New York: Simon & Schuster, 1994.

KATHARINE HATHAWAY: WRITER

Cravens, Gwyneth. "Past Present." *Nation,* October 25, 1993, Vol. 257, Issue 13, 472–474.

Hathaway, Katharine Butler. *The Little Locksmith.* New York: Coward-McCann, Inc., 1943.

Hathaway, Katharine Butler. *The Little Locksmith: A Memoir.* New York: Feminist Press at the City University of New York, 2000.

WALT DISNEY: CARTOONIST

Greene, Katherine and Richard Greene. *The Man Behind the Magic: The Story of Walt Disney.* New York: Viking Children's Books, 1998.

Thomas, Bob. *Walt Disney: An American Original.* New York: Simon & Schuster, 1976.

Thomas, Bob. *Walt Disney: Magician of the Movies.* New York: Grosset & Dunlap, 1966.

GLENN CUNNINGHAM: RUNNER

Cunningham, Glenn with George X Sands. *Never Quit.* Lincoln, VA: Chosen Publisher, 1981.

Lyttle, Richard B. *Challenged by Handicap.* Chicago: Reilly & Lee Books, 1971.

West, Ken. "Unforgettable Glenn Cunningham." *Readers' Digest,* November, 1988, 126–130.

ROY CAMPANELLA: CATCHER

Campanella, Roy. *It's Good to Be Alive.* Boston: Little, Brown & Company. 1959.

Macht, Norman L. *Roy Campanella: Baseball Star.* New York: Chelsea House Publishing, 1996.

Shapiro, Milton J. *Heroes Behind the Mask: America's Greatest Catchers.* New York: Julian Messner, 1968.

Van Riper, Guernsey. *Behind the Plate: Three Great Catchers.* Champaign, Illinois: Garrard Publishing Company, 1973.

BERNARD BRAGG: ACTOR

Bragg, Bernard as signed to Eugene Bergman. *Lessons in Laughter: The Autobiography of a Deaf Actor.* Washington, D.C.: Gallaudet University Press, 1989.

Powers, Helen. *Signs of Silence: Bernard Bragg and the National Theatre of the Deaf.* New York: Dodd, Mead and Co., 1972.

RAY CHARLES: MUSICIAN

Charles, Ray, and David Ritz. *Brother Ray: Ray Charles' Own Story.* New York: Da Capo Press, 1992.

Lydon, Michael. *Ray Charles: Man and Music.* New York: Riverhead Books, 1998.

ARTHUR ASHE: TENNIS PLAYER

"Arthur Ashe." *Current Biography.* New York: H.W. Wilson Co., 1996.

Ashe, Arthur, and Arnold Rampersad. *Days of Grace.* New York: Alfred A. Knopf, 1993.

Ashe, Arthur, and Neil Amdur. *Off the Court.* New American Library, 1983.

CHER: SINGER AND ACTRESS

"Cher." *Current Biography.* New York: H.W. Wilson Co., 1991.

"Cher." *People Magazine,* September 18, 2000.

Cher, with Jeff Coplon. *The First Time.* New York: Simon & Schuster, 1998.

Quirk, Lawrence J. *Totally Uninhibited: The Life and Wild Times of Cher.* New York: William Morrow and Company, Inc., 1991.

CONNIE BRISCOE: AUTHOR

Briscoe, Connie. *Big Girls Don't Cry.* New York: HarperCollins Publishers, 1996.

Briscoe, Connie. *A Long Way from Home.* New York: HarperCollins Publishers, 1999.

Briscoe, Connie. *Sisters & Lovers.* New York: HarperCollins Publishers, 1994.

"Connie Briscoe." *Current Biography,* January, 2000.

Southgate, Martha. "Speaking Volumes," *Essence,* July 1999, Vol. 30, Issue 3, 95–100.

Streitfield, David. "Connie Briscoe." *The Washington Post,* July 23, 1994.

ANN BANCROFT: EXPLORER

"Ann Bancroft." *Current Biography.* The H.W. Wilson Company, 2000.

Bancroft, Ann (with Nancy Loewen). *Four to the Pole!: The American Women's Expedition to Antarctica, 1992–1993.* North Haven, CT: Shoe String Press, Inc., 2001.

Martin, Katherine. *Women of Courage.* Novato, CA: New World Library, 1999.

Steger, Will, with Paul Schurke. *North to the Pole.* New York: Times Books, 1987.

Wenzel, Dorothy. *Ann Bancroft: On Top of the World.* Minneapolis: Dillon Press, 1990.

MARK WELLMAN: MOUNTAIN CLIMBER

Wellman, Mark, and John Flinn. *Climbing Back.* Waco, TX: WRS Publishing, 1992.

CHRIS BURKE: ACTOR

Burke, Chris, and Jo Beth McDaniel. *A Special Kind of Hero.* New York: Doubleday, 1991.

Italia, Bob. *Chris Burke: Star of "Life Goes On."* Edina, MN: Abdo & Daughters, 1992.

Lee, Gregory. *Chris Burke: He Overcame Down Syndrome.* Vero Beach, FL: Rourke Book Company, 1993.

Lamb 11

Deer 13

14   Moose

16   Zebra

Giraffe   17

18   Camel

Mouse   19

20 Squirrel

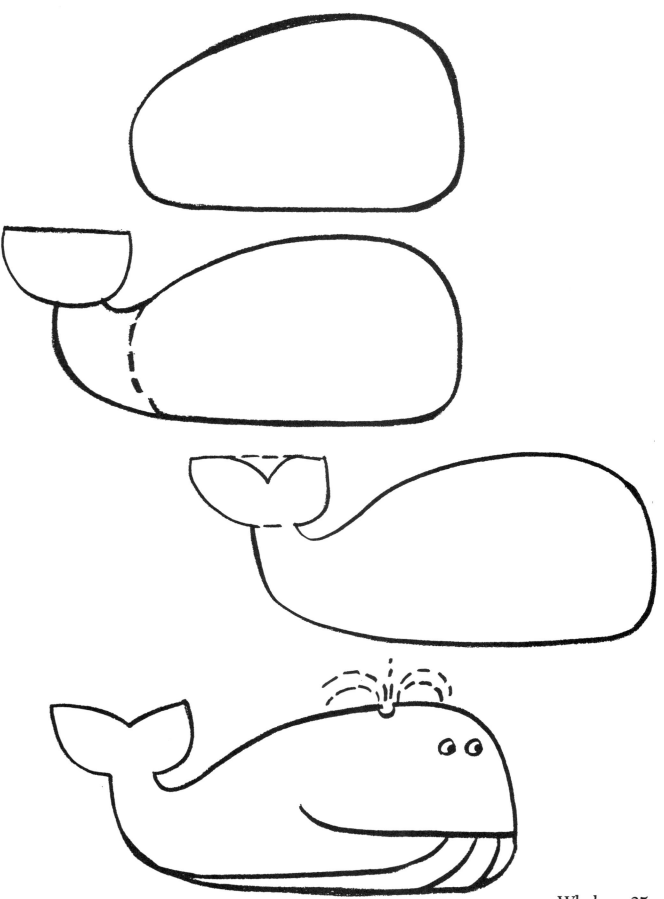

Bear 27

30   Chimpanzee

8　Dog

Leopard 7

6   Cat

Swan   5

4   Goose

Rooster   3

2   Duck

Chick   1

Note

Learning to draw your favorite animal is easier than it seems. By following the simple diagrams in this book, you can discover how to draw a smiling chimpanzee, a quacking duck, a hump-backed camel, and even a huge whale! Let's start with the picture of the chick on page 1 to show you how easy this can be. You will be doing some erasing, so use a pencil, not a pen. Start by drawing a large oval for the chick's body, with a small circle above for the head. Next, add the beak, the tail, and the outline of its wing, and erase the parts of the body indicated by the broken lines. Now, add the eye, the feathers on the wing, and finally the legs and feet. You've just drawn a chirping chick: wasn't that fun and easy? And there are 29 more animals to draw!

Copyright

Copyright © 1997 by Barbara Soloff Levy.
All rights reserved under Pan American and International Copyright Conventions.

Bibliographical Note

How to Draw Animals is a new work, first published by Dover Publications, Inc., in 1997.

Library of Congress Cataloging-in-Publication Data

Soloff Levy, Barbara.
    How to draw animals / Barbara Soloff Levy.
        p.   cm.
    ISBN 0-486-29867-1 (pbk.)
    1. Animals in art.   2. Drawing—Technique.   I. Title.
NC780.S62   1997
743.6—dc21   97–24315
                                                                CIP

Manufactured in the United States of America
Dover Publications, Inc., 31 East 2nd Street, Mineola, N.Y. 11501

How to Draw
ANIMALS

Barbara Soloff Levy

DOVER PUBLICATIONS, INC.
Mineola, New York

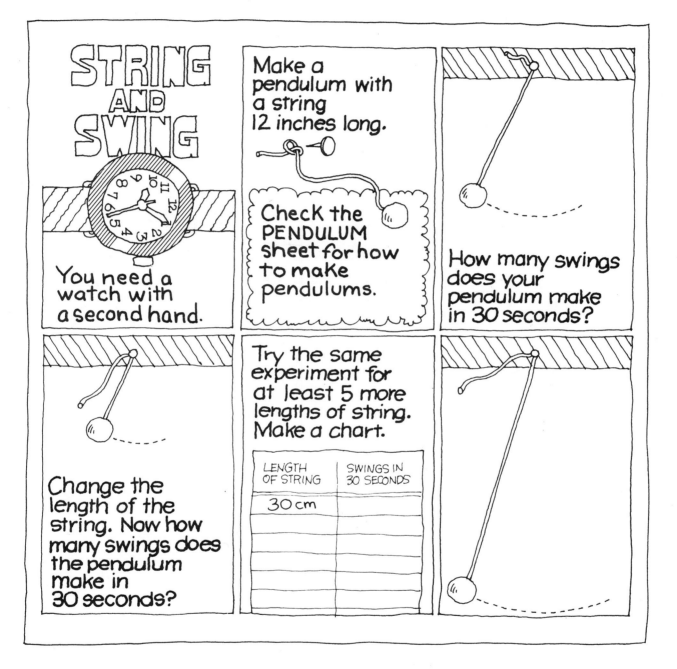

STRING AND SWING

You need a watch with a second hand.

Make a pendulum with a string 12 inches long.

Check the PENDULUM sheet for how to make pendulums.

How many swings does your pendulum make in 30 seconds?

Change the length of the string. Now how many swings does the pendulum make in 30 seconds?

Try the same experiment for at least 5 more lengths of string. Make a chart.

LENGTH OF STRING	SWINGS IN 30 SECONDS
30 cm	

In these activities, you use time to measure how pendulums can be made to swing at different rates.

Length of string	Swings in 30 seconds
30 cm	

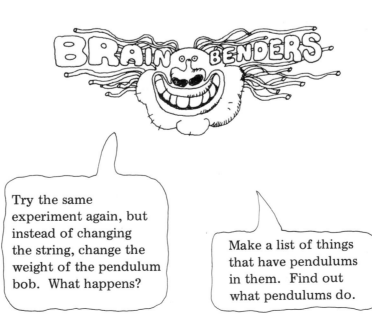

Try the same experiment again, but instead of changing the string, change the weight of the pendulum bob. What happens?

Make a list of things that have pendulums in them. Find out what pendulums do.

Statistics
and
Probability

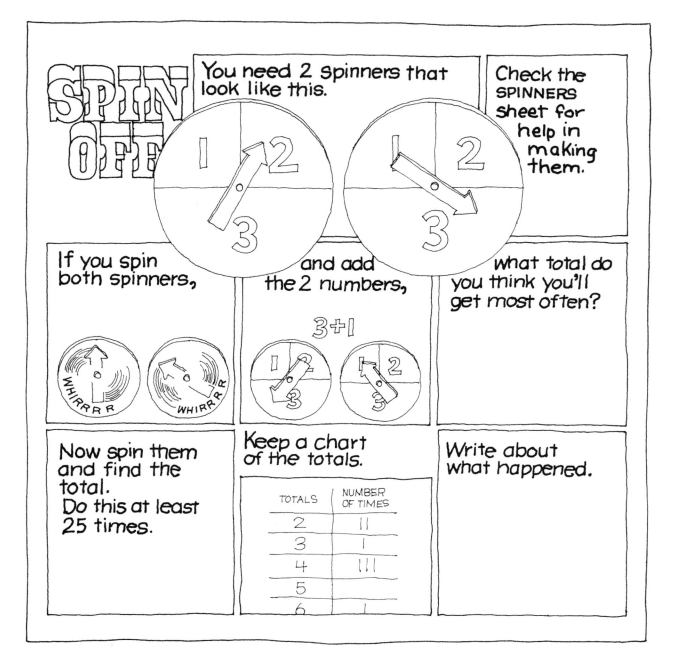

Probability is the study of how often something might happen. The best way to learn about probability is by experimenting first-hand. In this activity, you experiment with spinners.

Name . . . .

What total do you think you'll get most often?_____

Totals	Number of times
2	
3	
4	
5	
6	

What happened?_____

_____

_____

_____

_____

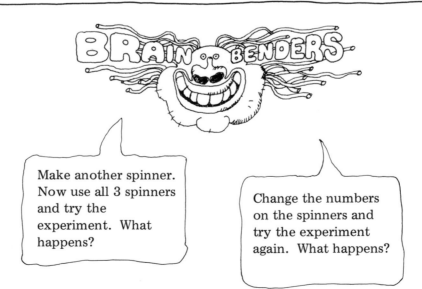

Make another spinner. Now use all 3 spinners and try the experiment. What happens?

Change the numbers on the spinners and try the experiment again. What happens?

Probability is the study of how often something might happen. The best way to learn about probability is by experimenting first-hand. In this activity, you experiment with dice.

Name . . . .

Fill this in before the game.

Players	Sums
	5, 6, 7, 8, 9
	2, 3, 4, 10, 11, 12

Keep a tally.

Sums	Number of times
5, 6, 7, 8, 9	
2, 3, 4, 10, 11, 12	

Who won? _____

BRAIN BENDERS

Change the game so that each player gets different sums. Guess who will win. Then try the game.

Change the rules of the game so that each player chooses just 1 sum. Score a point whenever your sum appears. Whoever scores 6 points first wins.

In these experiments, the probability of either heads or tails turning up is 50-50. You can also say the chance is 1 out of 2 or $\frac{1}{2}$. The more times you flip a penny, the closer you should get to exactly 50-50 results.

HEADS	TAILS

What happened after 10 flips?_____

What happened after 20 flips?_____

What happened after 100 flips?_____

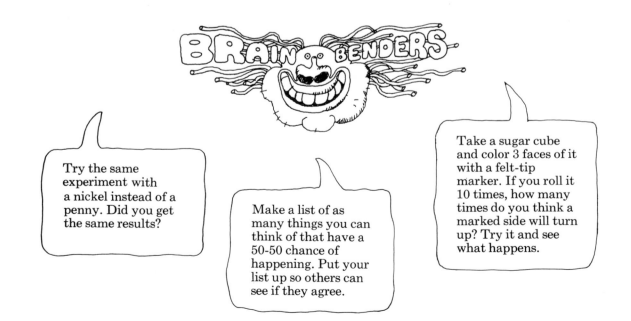

Try the same experiment with a nickel instead of a penny. Did you get the same results?

Make a list of as many things you can think of that have a 50-50 chance of happening. Put your list up so others can see if they agree.

Take a sugar cube and color 3 faces of it with a felt-tip marker. If you roll it 10 times, how many times do you think a marked side will turn up? Try it and see what happens.

In this experiment, it is hard to predict the chance of a thumbtack landing point-up until you try it.

Name . . . .

	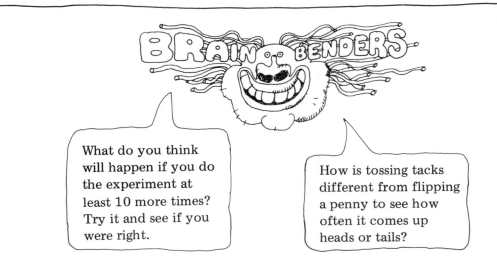	
1		
2		
3		
4		
5		
6		
7		
8		
9		
10		

What happened? _____

_____

_____

BRAIN BENDERS

What do you think will happen if you do the experiment at least 10 more times? Try it and see if you were right.

How is tossing tacks different from flipping a penny to see how often it comes up heads or tails?

Probability is the study of how often something might happen. The best way to learn about probability is by experimenting first-hand. In this activity, you experiment with spinners.

Name . . . .

Fill this in
before the game.

Players	Number chosen

Keep a tally.

Sums	Number of times
2	
3	
4	
5	
6	
7	
8	

Who won?_____

In this game does each
total have the same
chance of turning up?
Spin the spinners 100
times and mark the
sum each time. What
happens?

Change the game so
that each person picks
2 possible sums.
Score a point when-
ever either of your
sums appears.

For each suit in a deck of playing cards, 3 out of the 13 cards are face cards—Jack, Queen, and King. The chance or probability of a face card turning up if you deal a card is 3 out of 13, or $\frac{3}{13}$. What is the probability of a King turning up? How often should a red card turn up?

Name . . . .

HOW MANY FACE CARDS?

0	
1	
2	
3	
4	
5	
6	
7	
8	
9	
10	
11	
12	

What does the chart show?_____

_____

_____

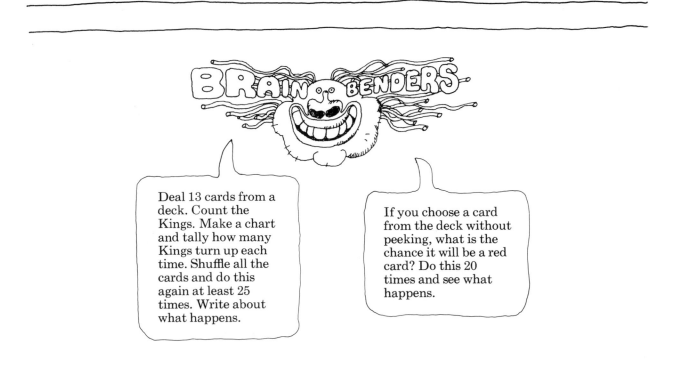

Deal 13 cards from a deck. Count the Kings. Make a chart and tally how many Kings turn up each time. Shuffle all the cards and do this again at least 25 times. Write about what happens.

If you choose a card from the deck without peeking, what is the chance it will be a red card? Do this 20 times and see what happens.

When you flip a penny and a nickel together, there are 4 possible combinations:

Name.....................................

What came up?	How many times?
Both heads	
Both tails	
One of each	

What happened?_____
_____
_____
_____

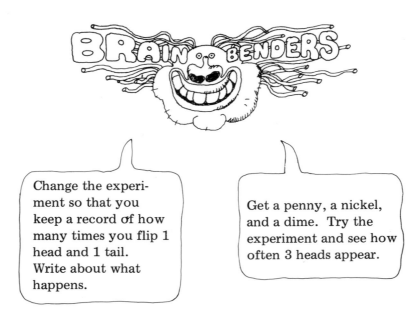

Change the experiment so that you keep a record of how many times you flip 1 head and 1 tail. Write about what happens.

Get a penny, a nickel, and a dime. Try the experiment and see how often 3 heads appear.

From the results of this experiment, you can learn about how often different letters are used in the English language.

Name ....

Keep a tally.

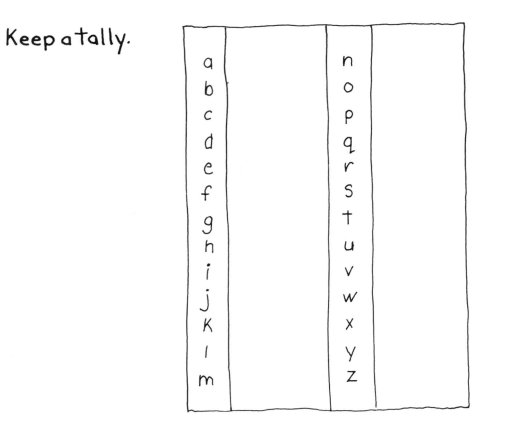

What does the chart show? _____

_____

_____

_____

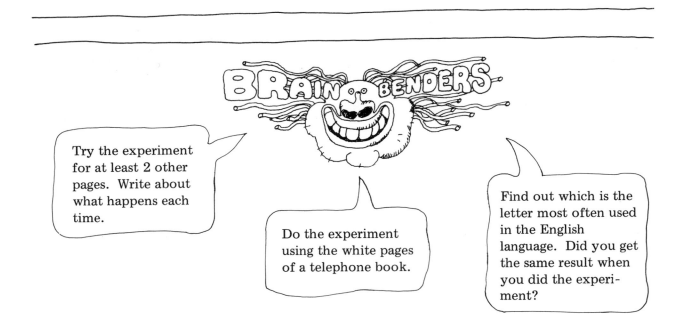

Try the experiment for at least 2 other pages. Write about what happens each time.

Do the experiment using the white pages of a telephone book.

Find out which is the letter most often used in the English language. Did you get the same result when you did the experiment?

When you make a survey, you collect information. This can be helpful when you are investigating a question. Information of this kind is called *statistics*.

Name . . . .

What survey are you making? _____

_____

Record your results here. _____

_____

_____

_____

_____

_____

_____

_____

BRAIN BENDERS

Out of 30 people, usually at least 2 have the same birthday. Make a survey and see if this happens in your class.

Make a survey about the entire school. Here are some ideas: How many children are absent each week? How many students have dogs? What is the average age of everybody in your school?

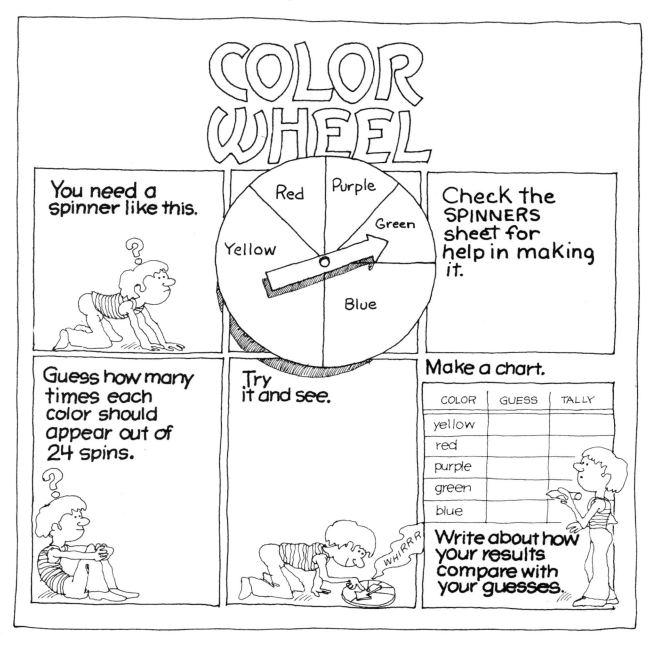

Probability is the study of how often something might happen. The best way to learn about probability is by experimenting first-hand. In this activity, you experiment with spinners.

Name ....

COLOR	GUESS	TALLY
Yellow		
Red		
Purple		
Green		
Blue		

How do your results compare with your guesses?

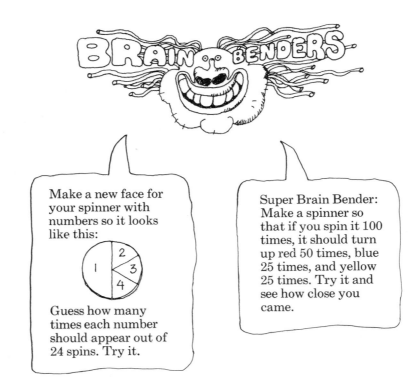

Make a new face for your spinner with numbers so it looks like this:

Guess how many times each number should appear out of 24 spins. Try it.

Super Brain Bender: Make a spinner so that if you spin it 100 times, it should turn up red 50 times, blue 25 times, and yellow 25 times. Try it and see how close you came.

SUMS	2	3	4	5	6	7	8	9	10	11	12
COMBINATIONS	1+1			1+4 2+3 3+2 4+1					4+6 5+5 6+4		

Probability is the study of how often something might happen. The best way to learn about probability is by experimenting first-hand. In this activity, you experiment with dice.

SUMS	2	3	4	5	6	7	8	9	10	11	12
COMBINATIONS	1+1			1+4 2+3 3+2 4+1					4+6 5+5 6+4		

What does the chart show?_____

_____

_____

_____

_____

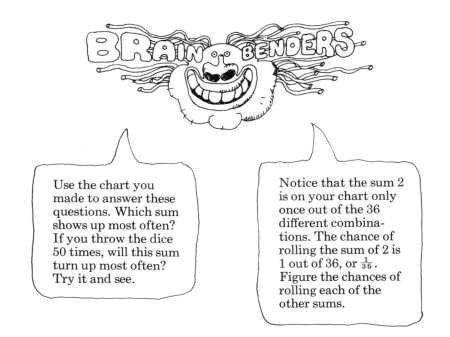

Use the chart you made to answer these questions. Which sum shows up most often? If you throw the dice 50 times, will this sum turn up most often? Try it and see.

Notice that the sum 2 is on your chart only once out of the 36 different combinations. The chance of rolling the sum of 2 is 1 out of 36, or $\frac{1}{36}$. Figure the chances of rolling each of the other sums.

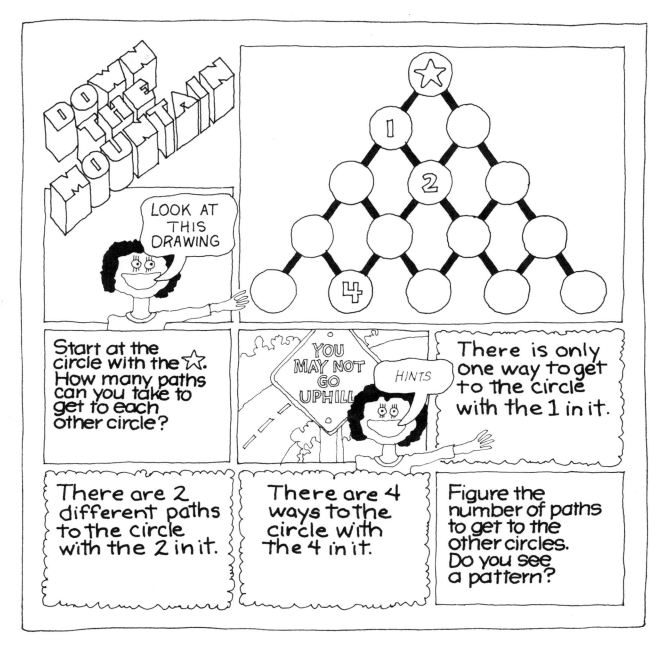

In this experiment, there are two possible paths from each circle. You investigate what happens when all of the possible paths are linked together. The pattern you get is *Pascal's Triangle*.

Name . . . .

Fill in each circle with the number of paths you can take to get to it.

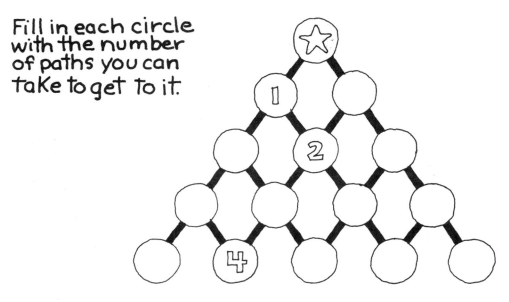

What are the patterns? _____

_____

_____

_____

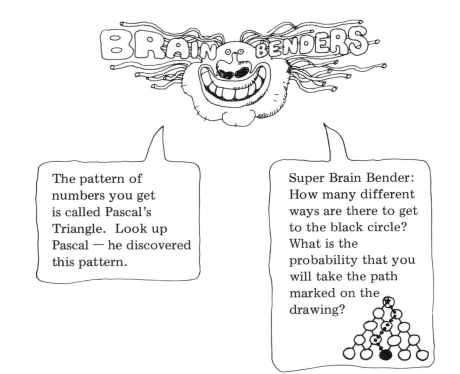

The pattern of numbers you get is called Pascal's Triangle. Look up Pascal — he discovered this pattern.

Super Brain Bender: How many different ways are there to get to the black circle? What is the probability that you will take the path marked on the drawing?

Collecting information in this experiment helps you learn about the length of words in the English language. This kind of information is called *statistics*.

Name . . . .

NUMBER OF LETTERS	WORDS	NUMBER OF LETTERS	WORDS
1		8	
2		9	
3		10	
4		11	
5		12	
6		more than 12	
7			

What does the chart show? _____

_____

_____

_____

_____

Use your results to answer these questions. How many letters were there in the longest word? Which length appeared most often? What is the average length of a word on the page you used?

Do you think the experiment would turn out differently if you used another book, a magazine, or a newspaper? Try it and see.

When you make a survey, you collect information. This can be helpful when you are investigating a question. Information of this kind is called *statistics*.

Name ....

Report your statistics here. _____

_____

_____

_____

_____

_____

_____

_____

_____

_____

_____

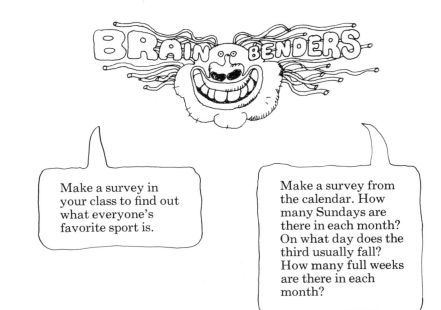

Make a survey in your class to find out what everyone's favorite sport is.

Make a survey from the calendar. How many Sundays are there in each month? On what day does the third usually fall? How many full weeks are there in each month?

In this activity, you organize information in order to find out how many different arrangements of things you can make.

Make a list of the possible committees.

EXAMPLE: 1, 2, 3
2, 4, 5
.
.
.

Change the problem so that you have 6 students to choose from. How many different committees could you make?

Suppose there were 3 people and 3 seats. How many different ways could the people be arranged? Try it with 4 people and 4 seats. How is this problem different from the others?

Functions
and
Graphs

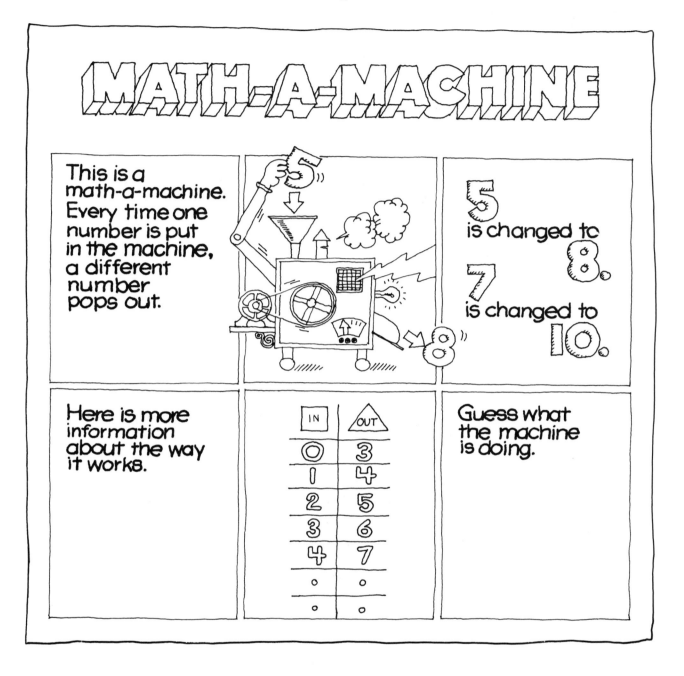

Seeing patterns is an important part of mathematics. In this activity, you investigate number patterns.

Name ....

Complete the chart.

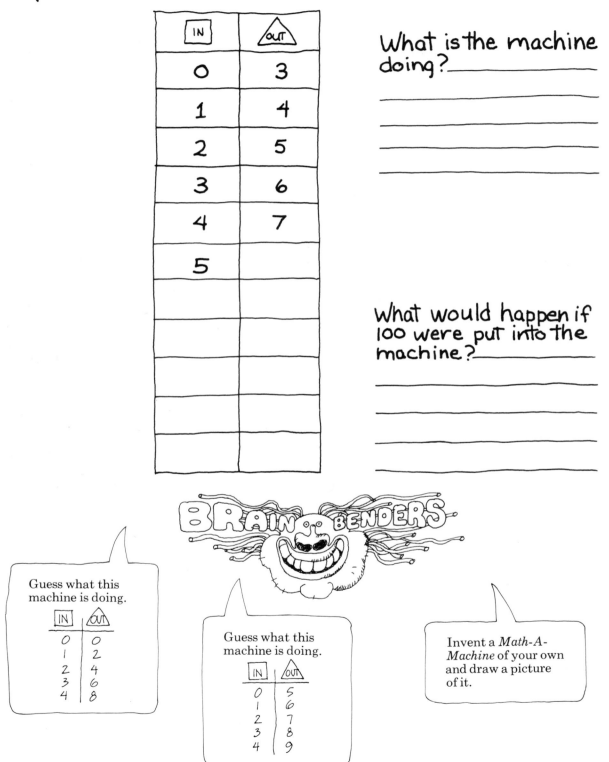

IN	OUT
0	3
1	4
2	5
3	6
4	7
5	

What is the machine doing?_____
_____
_____
_____
_____

What would happen if 100 were put into the machine?_____
_____
_____
_____
_____

BRAIN BENDERS

Guess what this machine is doing.

IN	OUT
0	0
1	2
2	4
3	6
4	8

Guess what this machine is doing.

IN	OUT
0	5
1	6
2	7
3	8
4	9

Invent a *Math-A-Machine* of your own and draw a picture of it.

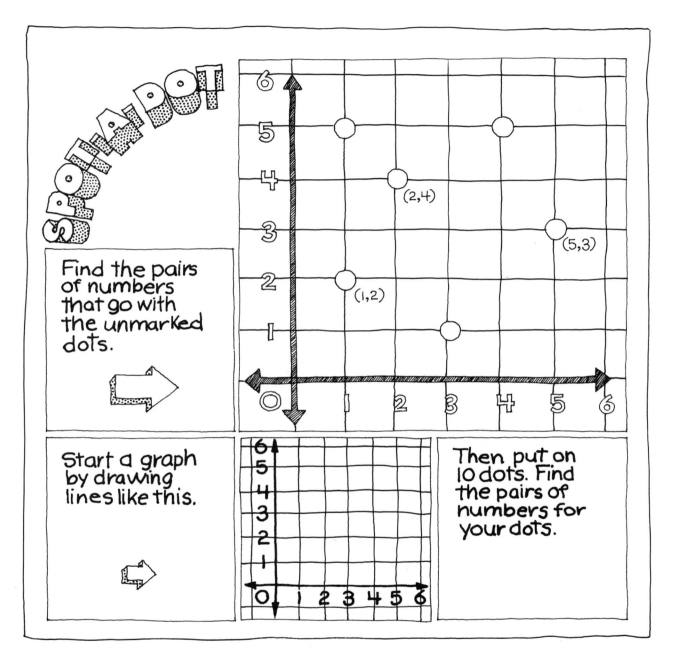

In this activity, pairs of numbers are used to put points on graphs. These pairs of numbers are the *coordinates* of a point.

Name ....

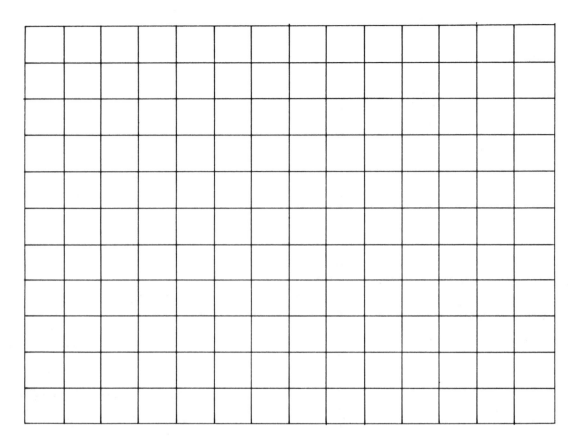

Find 5 pairs of numbers so that when you put them on your graph, all 5 dots will be in a straight line.

Find 4 pairs of numbers to put on your graph so that when you connect them, you form a square.

Play "4-in-a-row" on a graph. You need 2 players and another person to mark the dots on a graph. Taking turns, each player gives a pair of numbers to the marker. The marker records each pair of numbers on the graph. He uses an X for one player and an O for the other player. The winner is the first to get 4-in-a-row, $\begin{smallmatrix}o\\o\\o\\o\end{smallmatrix}$, xxxx, $^{oo}o_o$, or $_xx^{xx}$

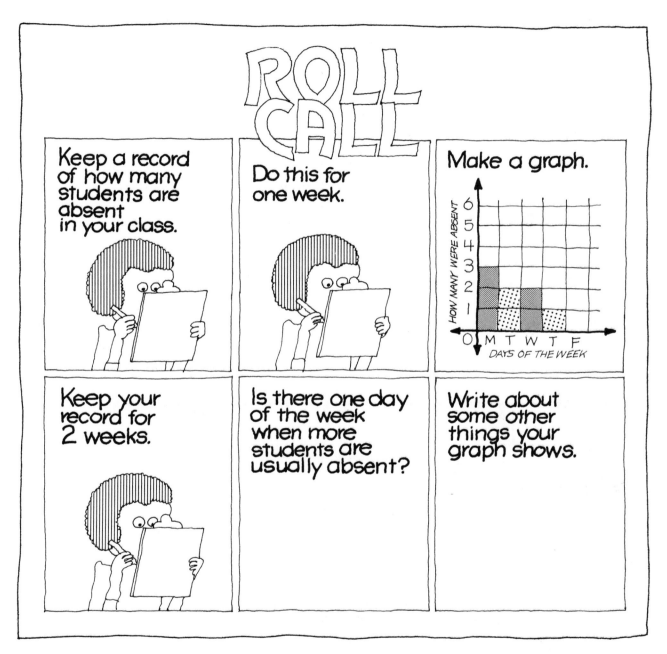

Graphs are a way to picture information. In this activity, graphs give you a clear and easy way to compare facts about your classmates.

Name . . . .

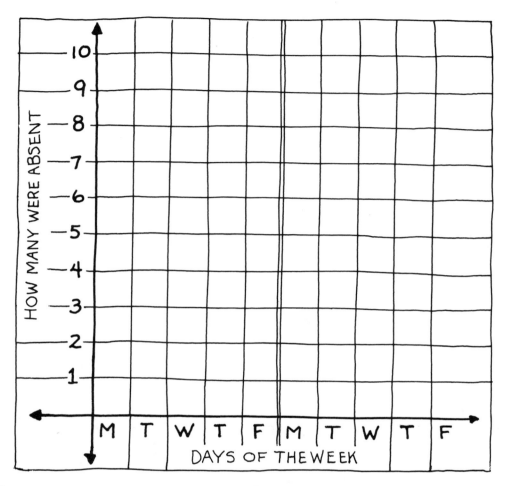

What does the graph show?

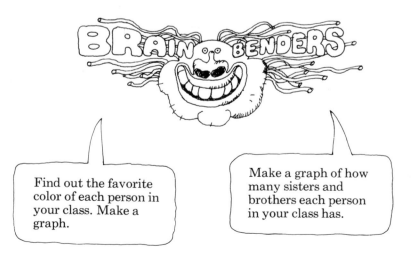

Find out the favorite color of each person in your class. Make a graph.

Make a graph of how many sisters and brothers each person in your class has.

Seeing patterns is an important part of mathematics. In this activity, you investigate number patterns which come from shapes that grow.

Name ....

How many in each square?

<u>1</u>

<u>4</u>

——

——

——

What patterns can you find?_____

_____

_____

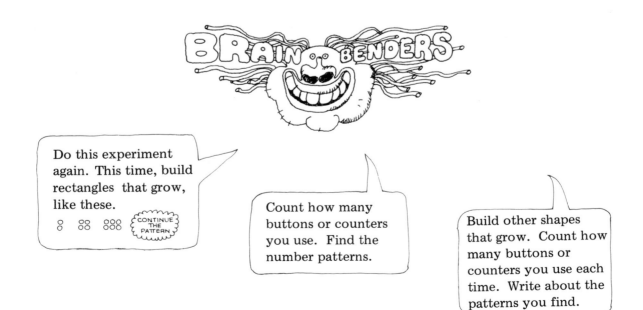

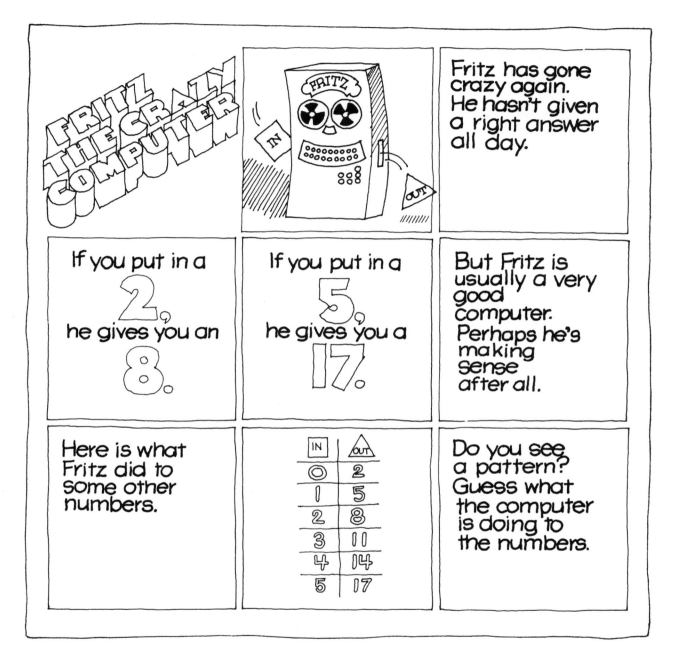

Seeing patterns is an important part of mathematics. In this activity, you investigate number patterns.

Name ....

Complete the chart.

IN	OUT
0	2
1	5
2	8
3	11
4	14
5	17
6	

What is the computer doing? _____
_____
_____
_____

What would happen if 100 were put into the computer? _____
_____
_____
_____
_____

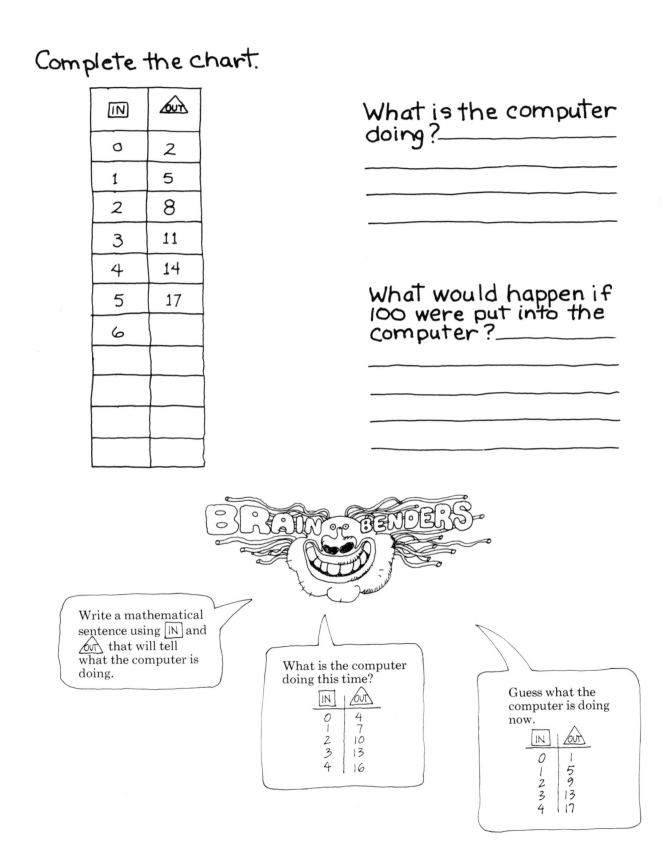

BRAIN BENDERS

Write a mathematical sentence using IN and OUT that will tell what the computer is doing.

What is the computer doing this time?

IN	OUT
0	4
1	7
2	10
3	13
4	16

Guess what the computer is doing now.

IN	OUT
0	1
1	5
2	9
3	13
4	17

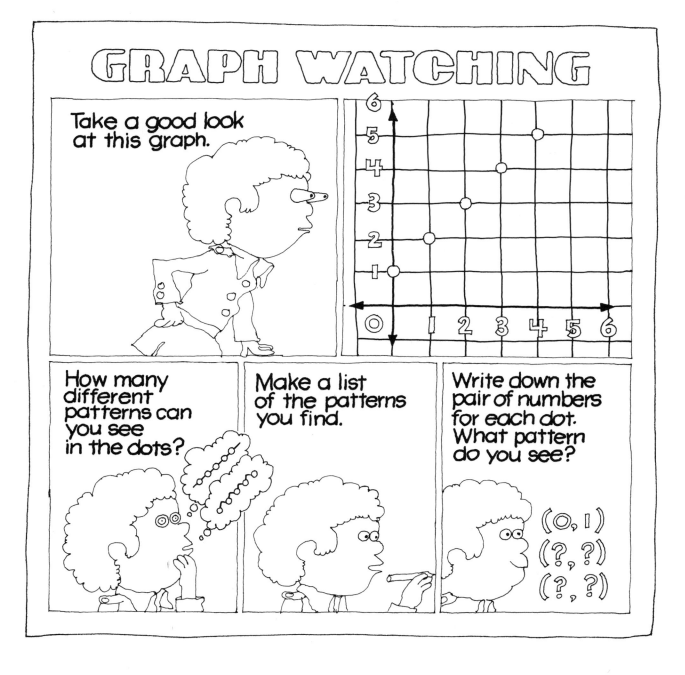

In this activity, pairs of numbers are used to put points on graphs. These pairs of numbers are the *coordinates* of a point.

Name . . . .

Write the pairs of numbers for each dot.

(0, 1)
(   )
(   )
(   )
(   )

What patterns do you see? _____

_____

_____

_____

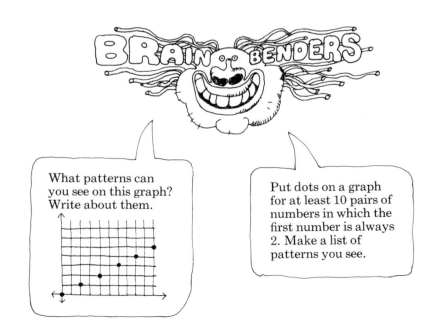

What patterns can
you see on this graph?
Write about them.

Put dots on a graph
for at least 10 pairs of
numbers in which the
first number is always
2. Make a list of
patterns you see.

Graphs are a way to picture information. In this activity, you graph patterns from arithmetic.

Name.....................................

Complete
the chart.

NUMBER	NUMBER × 2
0	0
1	2
2	4
3	
4	
5	
6	
7	
8	

Make
a graph.

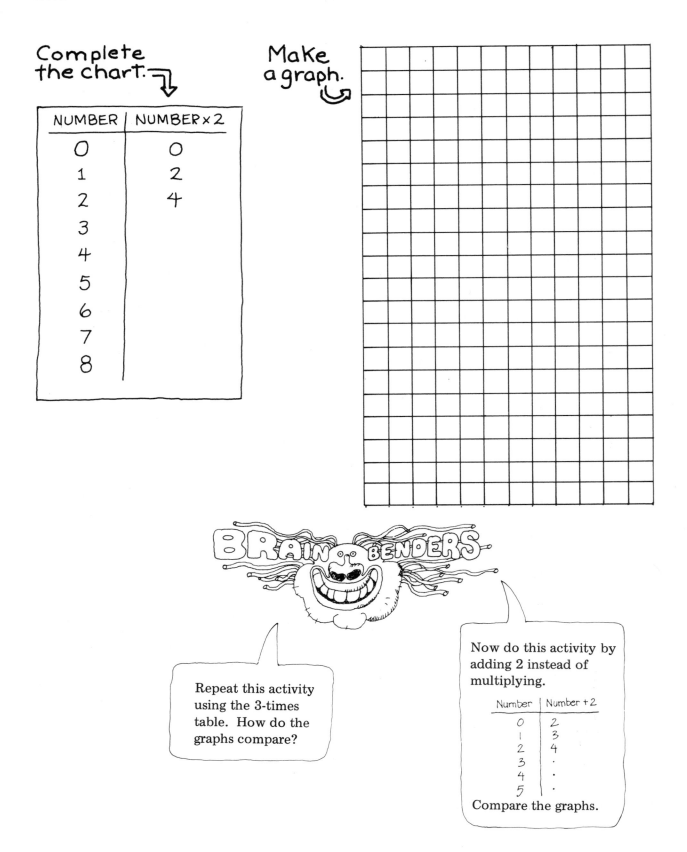

BRAIN BENDERS

Repeat this activity
using the 3-times
table. How do the
graphs compare?

Now do this activity by
adding 2 instead of
multiplying.

Number	Number + 2
0	2
1	3
2	4
3	.
4	.
5	.

Compare the graphs.

Seeing patterns is an important part of mathematics. Look carefully at the number patterns you get from these experiments.

Name ....

WIDTH IN SQUARES	LENGTH IN SQUARES

What patterns do you notice?_____

_____

_____

_____

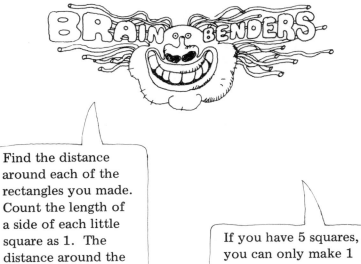

BRAIN BENDERS

Find the distance around each of the rectangles you made. Count the length of a side of each little square as 1. The distance around the rectangle is the *perimeter*. Is it the same each time?

If you have 5 squares, you can only make 1 kind of rectangle. For which other numbers of squares is this true?

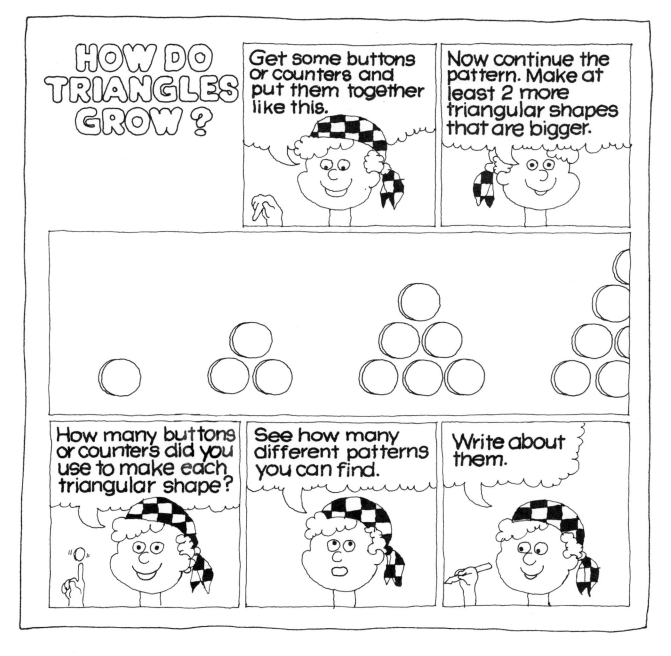

Seeing patterns is an important part of mathematics. In this activity, you investigate number patterns which come from shapes that grow.

Name.......................................

How many in each triangle?

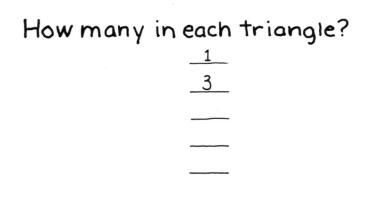

_1_

_3_

___

___

___

___

What patterns can you find?_____

_____

_____

_____

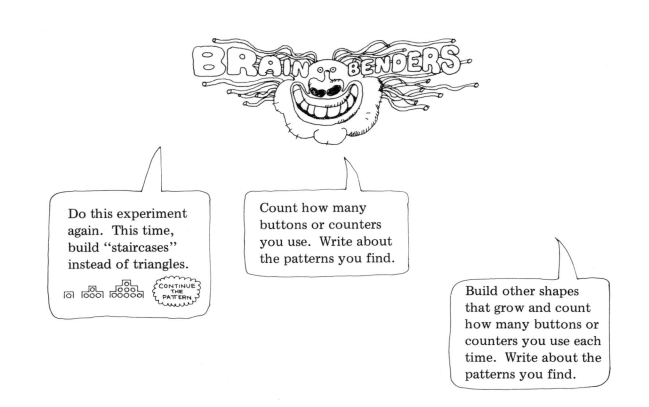

Do this experiment again. This time, build "staircases" instead of triangles. CONTINUE THE PATTERN

Count how many buttons or counters you use. Write about the patterns you find.

Build other shapes that grow and count how many buttons or counters you use each time. Write about the patterns you find.

Seeing patterns is an important part of mathematics. In this activity, you investigate number patterns.

Name . . . .

Continue the pattern.

0 ——→ 5

1 ——→ 7

2 ——→ 9

3 ——→ 11

4 ——→ 13

5 ——→ 15

6 ——→

7 ——→

8 ——→

9 ——→

10 ——→

What is the rule?

————————————————

————————————————

————————————————

————————————————

What would 100 change into?

————————————————

————————————————

————————————————

————————————————

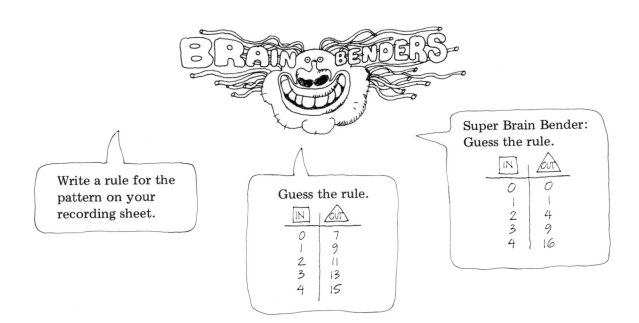

Write a rule for the pattern on your recording sheet.

Guess the rule.

IN	OUT
0	7
1	9
2	11
3	13
4	15

Super Brain Bender: Guess the rule.

IN	OUT
0	0
1	1
2	4
3	9
4	16

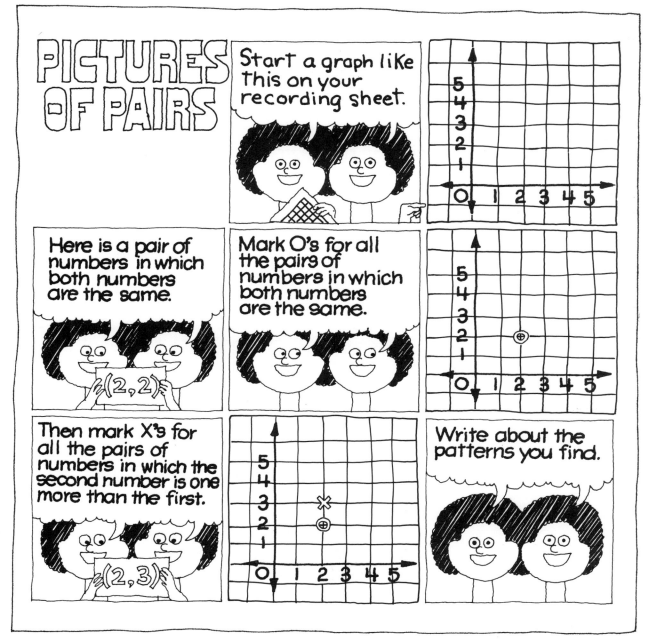

Graphs are a way to picture information. In this activity, you graph patterns from arithmetic.

Name . . . .

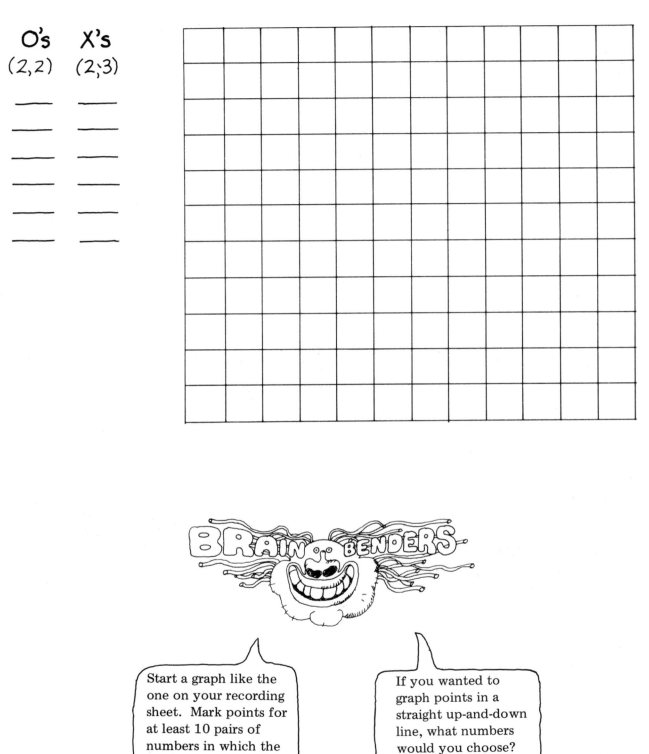

O's   X's
(2,2)   (2,3)

__ __ __

__ __ __

__ __ __

__ __ __

__ __ __

__ __ __

Start a graph like the one on your recording sheet. Mark points for at least 10 pairs of numbers in which the second number is always 4. Write about the patterns you find.

If you wanted to graph points in a straight up-and-down line, what numbers would you choose? Try it on a graph.

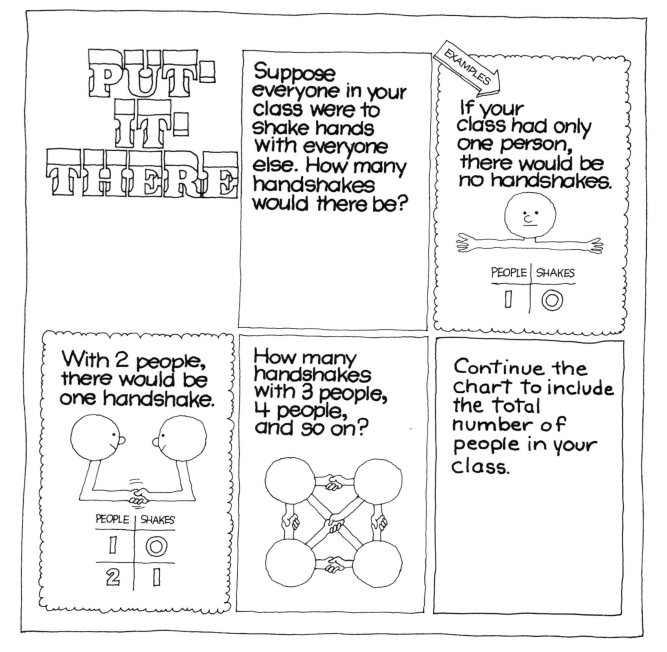

Seeing patterns is an important part of mathematics. This activity gives you number patterns to investigate.

Name . . . .

PEOPLE	SHAKES	PEOPLE	SHAKES
1	0	12	
2	1	13	
3		14	
4		15	
5		16	
6		17	
7		18	
8		19	
9		20	
10		21	
11		22	

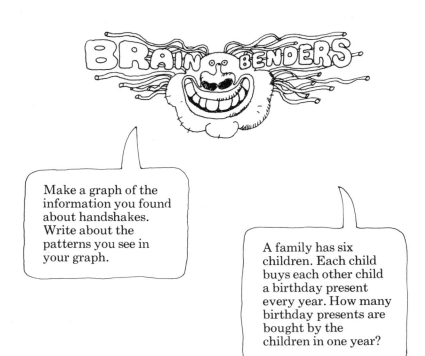

Make a graph of the information you found about handshakes. Write about the patterns you see in your graph.

A family has six children. Each child buys each other child a birthday present every year. How many birthday presents are bought by the children in one year?

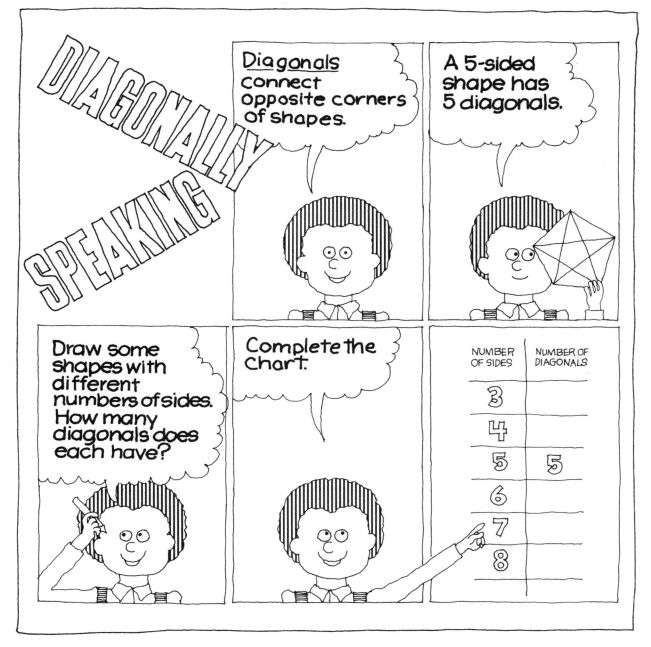

Seeing patterns is an important part of mathematics. Look carefully at the number patterns you get from these experiments.

Name ....

NUMBER OF SIDES	NUMBER OF DIAGONALS
3	
4	
5	5
6	
7	
8	

Draw your shapes here.

BRAIN BENDERS

Make a graph of the information you found on diagonals. Write about the patterns you see in your graph.

Look at the shapes you drew for your experiment. Count how many pieces the diagonals divide each shape into. Can you find a pattern?

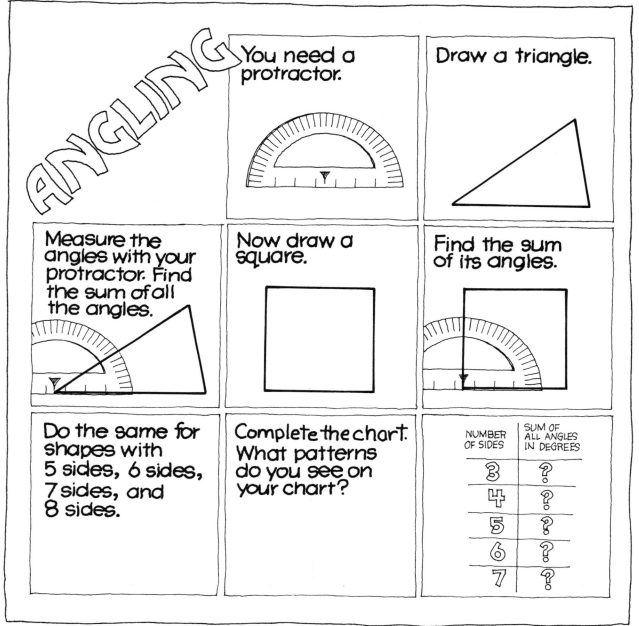

ANGLING

You need a protractor.

Draw a triangle.

Measure the angles with your protractor. Find the sum of all the angles.

Now draw a square.

Find the sum of its angles.

Do the same for shapes with 5 sides, 6 sides, 7 sides, and 8 sides.

Complete the chart. What patterns do you see on your chart?

NUMBER OF SIDES	SUM OF ALL ANGLES IN DEGREES
3	?°
4	?°
5	?°
6	?°
7	?°

Seeing patterns is an important part of mathematics. Look carefully at the number patterns you get from these experiments.

Event 70
Functions and Graphs
Angling

Name . . . .

NUMBER OF SIDES	SUM OF ALL ANGLES IN DEGREES
3	
4	
5	
6	
7	
8	

Draw your shapes here.

What patterns do you see? _____

BRAIN BENDERS

Draw at least 5 different triangular shapes. Now use your protractor to find the sum of the 3 angles in each. Write about what you find.

Draw at least 5 different 4-sided figures. Don't draw any with dents. Now use your protractor to find the sum of the 4 angles in each. Write about what you find.

Appendix

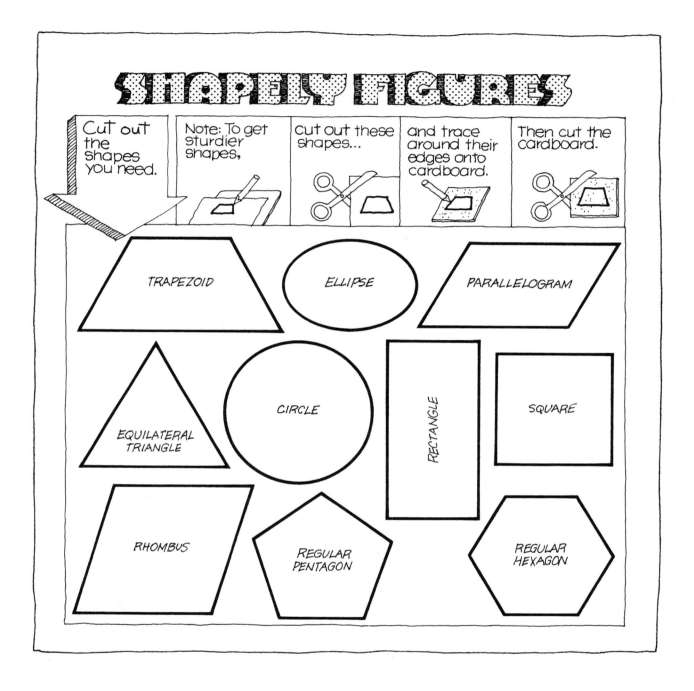

To be used for Events 5, 8, 11.

PENDULUMS

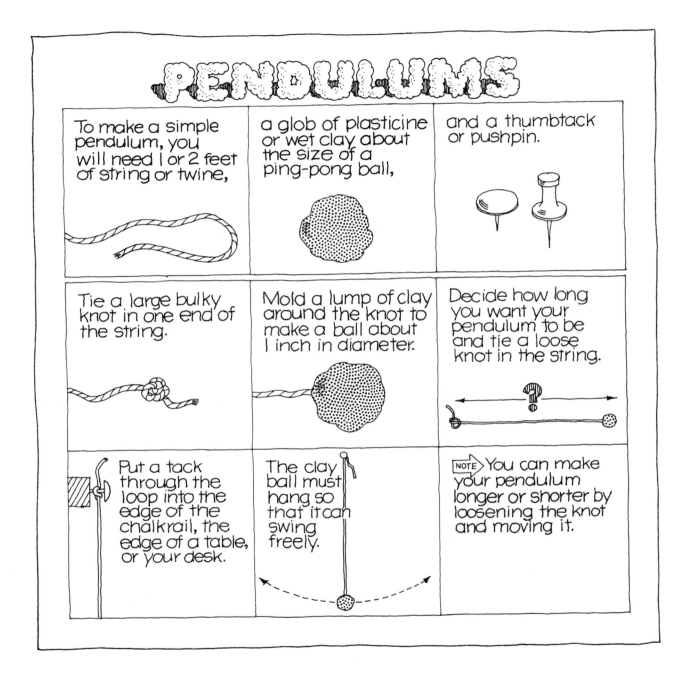

To make a simple pendulum, you will need 1 or 2 feet of string or twine,

a glob of plasticine or wet clay about the size of a ping-pong ball,

and a thumbtack or pushpin.

Tie a large bulky knot in one end of the string.

Mold a lump of clay around the knot to make a ball about 1 inch in diameter.

Decide how long you want your pendulum to be and tie a loose knot in the string.

Put a tack through the loop into the edge of the chalkrail, the edge of a table, or your desk.

The clay ball must hang so that it can swing freely.

NOTE> You can make your pendulum longer or shorter by loosening the knot and moving it.

To be used for Event 36.

SPINNERS

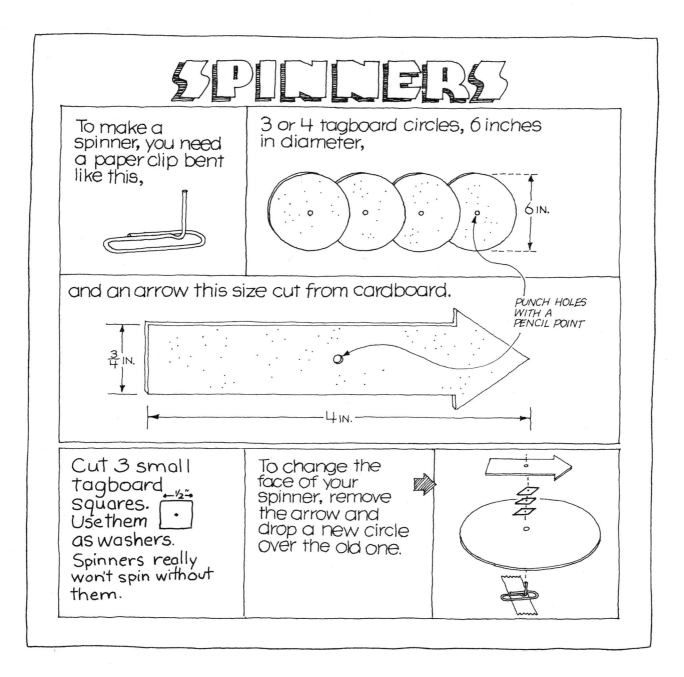

To make a spinner, you need a paper clip bent like this,

3 or 4 tagboard circles, 6 inches in diameter,

6 IN.

PUNCH HOLES WITH A PENCIL POINT

and an arrow this size cut from cardboard.

$\frac{3}{4}$ IN.

4 IN.

Cut 3 small tagboard squares. Use them as washers. Spinners really won't spin without them.

½"

To change the face of your spinner, remove the arrow and drop a new circle over the old one.

To be used for Event 37, 43, 49.